WHEN QUIETNESS CAME

A Neuroscientist's Personal Journey With Schizophrenia

Erin L. Hawkes, MSc

Library and Archives Canada Cataloguing in Publication

Hawkes, Erin L., 1979-
    When quietness came : a neuroscientist's personal journey with
schizophrenia / Erin L. Hawkes.

ISBN 978-0-9878244-4-8

    1. Hawkes, Erin L., 1979- --Mental health. 2. Schizophrenics--
Canada--Biography. 3. Neuroscientists--Canada--
Biography.
I. Title.

RC514.H39 2012   616.89'80092   C2012-901473-7

ISBN 978-0-9878244-4-8
First Published in 2012 by Bridgeross Communications, Dundas, Ontario, Canada

Disclaimer – Names have been changed

For my father,
who taught me the love of science,
and for my mother,
who taught me the love of books.

Acknowledgements

My first thanks is to my publisher and editor, Marvin Ross. Thanks for seeing the potential in the rough drafts and for believing it to be a story worth telling. Susan, thank you for connecting me with Marvin.

I am grateful for those friends who read the beginnings of this book and encouraged me to keep writing, particularly Cheryl, Jeff, Meghan, Ruth, and Sue. Your unjudging friendship is priceless.

Etta, I thank you for the hours of therapy, for witnessing and helping me cope with my emotions and my thoughts, my hopes and my fears. You gave me some of the strength I needed to put my story out for all to see. Thanks to the nurses and doctors at the hospitals who cared even when I gave them little reason to.

I dedicate this book to my parents with thanks for the support they give even when the illness wants me to push them away. Thank you for respecting my space and yet making me know that whenever I am ready, you are always there with love. Laura, thanks, too, for love and support I can really depend on.

And of course, my gratitude to Kassa for always being my rock when I doubt and my comfort when I am overwhelmed. Love is too little a word.

Table of Contents

Introduction

Dr. Richard O'Reilly MB FRCP (C), Professor, Department of Psychiatry, University of Western Ontario. London, ON, Canada

When Quietness Came describes what it is like to be mad. Some people will chastise me, a psychiatrist, for using the word mad, but madness is a commonly-used term for psychosis – to not be able to trust the reality of your senses or your thoughts – and I believe that clinical terms often sanitize and diminish the severity of these illnesses.

It is not acceptable in our society to be mad. There is a steep price to be paid for being psychotic: in your relationships, your career and in the pervasive infantilization and stigma that you may experience from others. These consequences of psychosis are accurately captured by Erin Hawkes in her account.

I recognize, from my own experience working with patients, the tyranny of psychotic symptoms described by Erin. Whatever perspective you hail from – patient, relative, friend, clinician, advocate – bear in mind Erin's description of her illness. Psychotic illnesses are not benign conditions; it is not "nice" to be mad! People suffer, and suffer greatly from their psychotic illnesses. Erin's first-hand account belies the callousness (it surely cannot be simple ignorance) of Thomas Szasz and groups such as Scientology who try to deny the existence of mental illness or flaky authors such as R.D. Laing who, when not blaming families for causing schizophrenia, imply that schizophrenia is simply a chance for introspection and personal development.

Erin, with her unique expertise as a neuroscientist and as a patient suffering from schizophrenia, tells us clearly that schizophrenia is a brain disorder and that its symptoms are related to disrupted levels of brain neurotransmitters.

Yet Erin makes the point that there is more to a person with schizophrenia than faulty neurotransmitter levels. We should not call people schizophrenic or regard them as "another case." Rather, Erin asks all of us to consider and respect the person with the illness. Erin's symptoms fluctuated with stress in her life. She found that reducing stress led to a decrease in her symptoms. However, Erin also found that clinicians and hospitals were reluctant to put much faith in her stress-relieving strategies and too often she ended up secluded or restrained.

I have to be honest and say that had I been her doctor, I would also have been prepared to restrain Erin to prevent her self-mutilation by severe head banging. But seclusion and restraint should be a last resort, used only when other interventions such as having capable nursing staff talk and spend time with patients do not work. A major barrier in implementing this simple approach is that cost-cutters have reduced budgets to levels where most psychiatric inpatient units are now understaffed.

Mental health services do not rely on the expensive high-tech machines or procedures that administrators seem to favour. Good mental health care requires sufficient numbers of competently trained professionals; a human resource that hospitals seem increasingly reluctant to fund.

I could not help noticing that Erin's symptoms did not respond well to numerous medications, and that only after much trial and error did her doctors find the "right drug." This is a story familiar to psychiatrists. Yet its meaning is overlooked. If all anti-psychotic medication blocks dopamine receptors – the common explanation of how they exert their therapeutic effect – why shouldn't every anti-psychotic at a sufficient dose not work to relieve every patient's psychotic symptoms?

In fact, anti-psychotic medications affect a number of different neurotransmitters apart from dopamine and different anti-psychotics have differential effects on each neurotransmitter. This diversity is responsible for the dissimilar side effects and may also account for the individuality of response to different drugs.

But a dose of humility is needed. We really do not know exactly how increased dopamine causes the symptoms of psychosis or how this might be modulated by other neurotransmitters. The brain is a vastly more complex organ than, say, the heart or liver, and even with our seemingly sophisticated tools we are only scratching the surface of understanding the brain. We need the brightest of our young minds to devote their lives to solving the persisting enigmas of schizophrenia. Early in her career, Erin showed that she was one of the brightest of young researchers. Years later, on effective medication, she is again participating in schizophrenia research.

I wish her every good fortune in fulfilling her dreams of making a significant contribution to the field of

Neuroscience. If that proves too difficult for Erin it surely emphasizes the need for a concerted effort to completely elucidate the cause of schizophrenia and to develop new treatments that can help people like Erin achieve a full recovery.

Chapter 1: Dying Time

I hadn't been feeling suicidal, really. It was more in response to what can only be called a Revelation that I decided to hang myself that Sunday in late September of 2001. I was puttering around my apartment when I saw the extension cord. I had seen it countless times before, I'm sure, but this time the sight of it flooded me with meaning. It had been foreordained, planned, and planted there for me to see, and I was gifted with the discernment to recognize the Deep Meaning – a mysterious, all-consuming, and bizarre alternate reality that my emerging psychosis created and convinced me of – behind its simple material substance. The Voices, whispering at first, but steadily increasing in both volume and intensity, drew me into that Deep Meaning.

"It's time," They informed me. "Time to die, dying time. The girl dies, the girl dies!" It made sense to me; a feeling of Rightness inundated my heart and mind. "She dies, she dies, she dies." Of course – I had survived my previous suicide attempts in order to wait for the true time, the perfect timing of a Meaning so profound I could barely discern its message.

The Voices became more insistent, slipping into their usual obscene language and derogatory litanies. "Hang her, you fucking bitch," the Voices commanded, speaking both to me and about me. "Piece of shit, die, girl, die." Male and female young and old, the Voices chorused together. Louder, louder, till they overwhelmed my senses and tore me from what shreds of reality to which I had until then still clung. *I don't want to die,* my rational side, the side that pursued studies in Neuroscience, had whispered to me at first, but by now it had been silenced by the more powerful hallucinations and delusions of my nascent schizophrenia. "She dies! The girl hangs!" This was the Truth; this was Revelation.

High, as it were, on my psychosis, I felt a tremendous sense of Rightness as I fashioned a noose out of the extension cord. But where to hang it from? I waited, glancing around the room, for further instruction. Ah, the metal V-shaped door closer that jutted invitingly out above the door. I tested its strength: sufficient. Using another cord, I attached the noose securely, made sure that it was high enough off the floor so as to be able to hang. Voices were shouting so loudly at me. "Die, die, die," They yelled. Obediently, I put the noose around my neck. *I won't kick the chair away,* I thought as I stepped carefully off it. *I don't want the apartment to look messy when they find me.*

The noose tightened. Gasping, I felt my head go light and my vision turn dark. "I come to you," I whispered to the Voices.

"Die, die, die! The girl dies! Hang her, kill her, bitch. You are coming to us." Deep peace washed over me. I was fulfilling such a cosmic destiny, aligning myself with the Deep Meaning of the universe.

But then peace turned to panic. My vision blurred, and all of a sudden I saw it clearly. I was outside my body, standing a few feet away, watching this girl hang herself. *That's me*, I realized. I am going to die! To hell with the Plans and Voices – I was going to die. I had only seconds left before I'd pass out and hang till death. What was more important: my obedience to the Voices of death, or my desperate instinct to survive?

"Don't you dare stop, bitch! Die, girl, die! Come on, come on – you're almost there. The Plan will be fulfilled and you will come to us. The girl dies!"

I couldn't. I wanted to live, and the shock of realizing that I was really and truly about to die threw me back into reality. I felt for the chair, stepped on, and stood there gasping for air. Voice whirled around me, through me, but I didn't care. I wanted to live. Fuck the Voices and Their Plans; I was going to live.

In time I removed the noose from my neck. Trembling, exhausted, and so shook up that I all but ignored the shouted tirade of the Voices, I fled to my bed. It was only mid-afternoon, but I fell into a deep sleep.

When I awoke later that evening, the Voices had settled down and my mind had cleared. I could remember everything vividly, and it terrified me. If my absurd sense of orderliness had not kept me from doing the traditional kick-the-chair-away hanging, I would have been unable to save myself, I realized. Then, the scariest thought: it could happen again. I knew that the Voices, with Their convincing Plans and insistent commands, would be back – They always came back. Finally, after years of thinking that I would always win, I knew that this was stronger than what I could handle on my own. I needed help.

I remembered the little form we had filled out the

other Sunday, the one with the box that you could tick for "Yes, I'd like to meet with the pastor." Too shy to phone, I sent an email. Subject: "From the quiet one:"

Yes, I'd like to meet with the pastor... I just keep struggling to see enough purpose in life to keep living. Surely there must be, but the quiet voice that says so need only be silenced for the short minute it takes to kill oneself – and all is lost.

Erin

A reply came quickly:

Hi Erin:

I would love to meet with you! I am available anytime Monday, Tuesday after 2:30 P.M., Thursday before 11:00 A.M. Feel free to e-mail a time that is good for you. I can travel to where you are! In the meantime hang in there!

God bless,
Brian

Hang in there. *How appropriate,* I thought wryly. That expression tore through me. I felt so scared, so alone. I reached for the phone and dialled my friend Yaliel's number. *Please be home,* I prayed.

"Hi, is Yaliel there, please?"

"Just a second, I'll go check."

"Hello?"

"Hi, it's Erin. I – I just…. Oh, I don't know how to say this. It's just that…. I tried to hang myself today. And I'm scared. Really scared."

"Oh, Erin, no. Are you okay for a few minutes? I'll

come right over."

"Yeah, I'm okay now. Thanks."

"Okay, I'll be over in ten minutes. Hang in there, Erin."

"Bye." *Hang in there.* Again. How did such an expression become such a part of our everyday language? So familiar that no one thinks about what those words might imply. Hang in there. Right.

True to his word, Yaliel was over as quickly as he could. I broke down, crying on his shoulder while he shushed me like a little girl and held me tight. All the built-up emotion from the day – from the weeks, months, and years – flowed down my cheeks. Why had it come to this? And where would it go next?

After a while I calmed down, and patted my eyes dry. Sensing that I had wept through the worst of it, Yaliel broke the silence. "You need help, Erin," he said gently.

"I know," I whispered. Finally, it had become so big, so monstrous, so absolutely terrifying that I could no longer pretend that if I just tried hard enough, I would win. I was broken, and no longer believed the lie that I could mend myself.

"Tomorrow, you can go to the psychological counselling service on campus," he suggested. "They'll know how to help you."

"Okay." I was emotionally exhausted. I would go. *Yes, I'll be alright overnight,* I assured Yaliel. So he left, and I crawled back to my bed and embraced the oblivion of sleep.

True to my word, I went first thing the next morning to Dalhousie University's counselling and psychological services. "Can I help you?" asked a sympathetic receptionist. I was upset, scared about the fact that I was going through the motions of getting my secret battles told.

"Yes, I, um, need to see someone," I said, my voice barely above a whisper.

"There's no openings for a couple days. Or, is it an emergency?"

"I – I really need to see someone today."

"Okay, we keep a few spots open for emergencies. How about this afternoon, around 4:00?"

"I have class…."

"Then it's not an emergency," the receptionist said, but kindly.

"No; I mean, yes. Yes, 4:00."

"Okay. Your appointment is with Patti."

"Thanks." I clutched at the appointment card she handed me, reading it as if from very far away. Patti. 4:00.

*   *   *

"I have to leave early," I informed my professor. It was a small, fourth-year Neuroscience laboratory techniques course with just nine students, and absences required valid excuses. *Like hanging in there*, I reasoned to myself. Sparing her the details, I just said it was an urgent doctor's appointment.

Yaliel was also in the class. He arrived late, as usual. He looked at me, asking me with his expression how I was. I flashed the appointment card at him. He smiled, and gave a thumbs-up.

At ten to four, I left. My heart was racing, pounding. *I have an appointment with Patti, at 4:00*; the receptionist remembered me. Waiting room. I held my head in my hands, beaten.

"Erin?" Patti was a middle-aged woman, neatly tucked in, small shoes, quiet voice. Mousy, but in a sympathetic fashion. I followed her down the hall to her office. "What can I do for you?" she asked as we sat down.

15

After a few moments of my silence passed, she prodded me gently. "What brought you here today?" The classic first-meeting questions. And the answers? Those I had to supply.

"I had a bad day yesterday," I began tentatively. She waited. "I – I tried to hang myself." I didn't mention the Voices; I thought they were a given, that everyone experienced them. The only difference was that they could function with them. That the suicide attempt was in accordance with Their Plans I also kept to myself; no one was to know the Deep Meaning but me.

I knew that this suicide attempt was serious but her expression and tone of voice made me realize that it was even more so than I had thought. She drew me out, quietly but persistently. I don't remember what all I said. All I knew was that I was transferring some of the burden of all that I had been through onto someone else. *Help me*, I pleaded silently.

As the hour drew to a close, Patti had to make a decision about me. Unsure of what would be in my best interest, she asked me to come back after hours, so that she could help me figure out a plan for the night.

I was restless, full of emotion. Voices returned periodically, at times constant. "What the fuck do you think you're doing? Piece of shit, you're not worth Patti's time. You just try and stop us. You'll never win. Our Plans rule – you stupid, stupid girl, to think you could escape our grasp. We win – the girl dies!" On and on and on. I wept for quietness.

Patti suggested the hospital, but I balked. I wasn't that sick, I thought; after all, I had attempted suicide before and all I had needed were a few Band-Aids on my wrists. "But can you promise me you'll be okay tonight?" she insisted.

I hated to admit defeat, but I knew how powerful the Voices and their Plans could be – and that they could return in full force at any moment. "No, I can't."

"Is there anyone you could stay with? If not, I really feel that you should be in hospital."

I thought about the people in the city I could count on, but due to my building schizophrenia and its accompanying social deficits, I had no friends but Yaliel. My pastor? Brian was welcoming; he had made it clear that I could count on him. We were going to meet up the next day anyway as the result of my email so I called.

Patti kept me with her until around 9:00 that night, then left me waiting for Brian. I sat in the dark outside the Student Union Building (SUB), at once scared about what had happened and the possibility of it happening again and yet also calm, knowing that I had initiated contact with people who would help me through this.

I spent a restless night at Brian's, sleeping in my clothes on the couch. We talked some – enough for Brian and his wife to get an idea of how desperate the situation was. My mood was black, fed by the Voices' derogatory comments about me and their views on my life. *Why bother to live?* I asked myself. *What's the point?* Or, rather, was there more Meaning in suicide than in simply living? Suicides shake people up, I reasoned, make them live more fully, more deliberately. "Your destiny is to die," the Voices reminded me. "The Great Plan. Don't think you can live when you are the one chosen to live a Deep Meaning by dying. The girl dies!"

*   *   *

"May I help you?" Another receptionist. Another plea for an emergency appointment. Another link to moor

17

me in the sea of sanity and health.

"I need to see a doctor. Patti from psychological services said she would call about me?" She had; *could I have a seat, and the doctor will see you shortly?* I had promised Patti I would come to Student Health Services this next morning. Perhaps some medication would help? In retrospect, I see that Patti wasn't in a position to be the sole professional responsible for such a case as mine. *Erin? I'm Dr. Pannel. Follow me, please.* I stood, I walked, I followed.

"I talked with Patti this morning, Erin, but I'd like to hear what happened from you."

"I tried to hang myself," I stated bluntly. Patti mustn't have mentioned the details, as I noticed the doctor flinch at my statement. She had some questions, and I extended some answers. What was she going to do with me? Some pills? She mentioned antidepressants.

She continued, as I struggled to pay attention. Then one word sliced through my ears and pierced my brain.

"…hospital. I'll go make some calls. Be right back."

Hospital? No – I would be fine. Not the hospital. But what could I do but wait for her to come back? Surely the hospital people would see that my case wasn't so serious. Just an attempted suicide, that's all. Commonplace stuff. Doesn't everyone have suicide plans? She's back – what's she saying? The NS? The hospital my friend's crazy friend spent time at? "I called Queen Elizabeth II Hospital, but you live in a district covered by the Nova Scotia Hospital, so I'm sending you there. Do you have someone who could drive you there, or should I call a cab?"

Brian had said that if I needed any help today I could call him – he was available until mid-afternoon. Again, hating my dependency but thankful for his sincere offer to help me, I dialled his number. He came, and we left. He laid, on the dash, the sealed enveloped the doctor had given him to give to the admitting nurse at the NS. What was written about me?

The nurse was expecting us when we arrived. It was my initiation into the mental health system, where notes and reports and discussions are shared between professionals and hidden from the patient, where diagnoses and assumptions go before me and remain a trail behind me. Welcome to psychiatry.

They put me on the Short Stay unit, a quiet ward with almost more nurses than patients that night. *So it's come to this*, I thought. Was it a relief, finally relinquishing my illusion of control and sanity? Or was it a prison, entrapping me in the narrow confines of the mental health care system? I didn't know. One thing I did know: I had to tell my parents. The objective criterion for mental problems – being admitted into a psychiatric hospital – had transpired, and I really couldn't keep them in the dark any longer.

"Hello?"

"Hi, Dad. It's Erin. Is Mom around, too?" If I was going to do this, I wanted to only do it once, to them both at the same time.

"I'll go tell her you're on the line." A few eternal seconds passed. "Hi, Erin."

"Hi. I have some bad news to tell you," I began. *Focus on the objective, Erin.* The facts. "I'm in the hospital." Gasps, oh no's, what happened's, why's.... I took a deep breath, wished my heart's pounding to stop, and kept my voice steady. "Attempted suicide." No feelings, just that plain fact.

There can never be words to capture what my parents must have felt in that instant, no words for any parent who hears those words – or worse, hears the words "your child" and "suicide" without the word "attempted." I don't remember what they said, but they wanted to come down to Halifax right away, that night. But I could barely handle talking to them over the phone, let alone deal with them in person. *Not tonight, please. Tomorrow, if you must.* They ached to do something, anything, and here I was not wanting to see or even talk with them. It was just too much for me.

*   *   *

My first night sleeping in those blue hospital pyjamas came and went, but I had no appetite for breakfast. *This is it.* Emotions pulled me in so many directions. Fear and relief, peace and anxiety. *I will let them help me.* What would it be like, staying a couple days in a psychiatric hospital? Would it really make a difference? Was this finally the bottom and things could only get better from here?

Soon my parents were there. "...so you see, we'd like to keep her here a couple of days. Observe her, try her on some medication." My first of innumerable psychiatrists was talking with my parents and me in a sunny interview room. I gazed out the window, dissociated from my body. Keep her? I tuned into the conversation. A few days? "...probably not more than a week or two," he continued. What? I couldn't stay here that long. I wasn't that sick – I had only attempted suicide, after all – and besides, I had classes and labs to go to.

Some official papers were presented to me. "Sign here," the psychiatrist prompted. "It's to say that you are being admitted voluntarily."

"But I don't want to stay here that long," I protested.

"If you don't sign in as a voluntary patient, I might

20

have to certify you."

"Certify?"

"It means that you haven't committed yourself voluntarily while a psychiatrist deems hospitalization necessary; more specifically, if you try to leave, we have the legal right to have the police escort you back to hospital. Certification is usually valid for a week, then it's often renewed for a month. But believe me, it's better that you admit yourself voluntarily."

"But why?"

"Just for the record." I still didn't see his point. After all, I reasoned to myself, although a voluntary patient could in theory sign themselves out at any point, couldn't a psychiatrist just counter their attempt to leave with a certification? Yet I was emotionally exhausted by this point. If he wanted me to sign, then I would sign. "There now. Good. We're just waiting for a bed at this point. She'll be moved up to one of the acute care wards as soon as possible," he said, directing his words towards my parents.

As soon as possible came later that day. They pulled me from the quiet Short Stay ward and brought me up to a busy ward on the third floor. Laurel, it was called. Visibly more crazy. Could I use that word now – now that I was a "crazy" myself? A nurse showed me around, and introduced me to my quiet roommate. "Ellen, this is Erin." Neither of us was feeling very social at that point. Actually, Ellen was never social. I'm not exactly sure why she was there, but she certainly wasn't well. Depressed, maybe? But something more than that; she was weirder than "ordinary folk."

Supper came and went, but I still had no appetite. I paced the length of the ward, up and down, back and forth, one end to the other. I stood at the west-facing window, watching a beautiful sunset filter through the bars locking me in. Then at the east end, I looked through the locked door's window into the ward across the hall. Mayflower seemed even wilder than Laurel, I noted. A classic pyjama-clad crazy danced down the hall and sang out loud. I turned back to my pacing. Another circuit; I read the sign posted on the door. "Risk of elopement. Door temporarily locked to ensure patient safety." Yes, but "temporarily," I soon came to know, really meant "all the time." And elopement was no marriage; it meant we crazies might make run for it given half a chance. So visitors, kindly make sure that the damn door locks behind you. Such is life on a locked psych ward.

After I tired of the pacing, I sat in the dining room sipping warm water quietly by myself. Then: "Hi. You're new here. My name's Jay." I looked up, and he sat down. "First time? Did they certify you? What're you in for? You look normal enough; heck, at first I thought, Hey, a new nurse. But then you're in the room with Ellen, so I figured you were a patient." I nodded to the first question, shook my head to the second, and tried to take in all he was saying. He sure was a talker, I quickly realized. A talker was at least a distraction.

"... yeah, so what're you in for?" he asked again with a know-it-all's curiosity. Too tired for many words, but sensing that he'd ask the question a hundred times in order to get an answer, I said bluntly, "I tried to hang myself."

"Oh, not a pretty girl like you." Was this a compliment or disbelief? At this point, I hardly cared.

Jay was starting into another soliloquy when a new admission sat down. I glanced up and lost myself in grey-blue eyes that seemed to see right into my soul. Brenden Porter; a fellow troubled youth, perhaps? Artsy type for sure, and as hungry as I was for connection in this strange place. Jay prattled on. "You guys sure are connecting," he commented at one point. I was surprised he could be so observant, given the amount of energy it must have taken him to keep up his constant chatter. A bit miffed at both Brenden's and my lack of attention to his stream-of-consciousness speech, he left.

"Attempted suicide," I answered to Brenden's unspoken question. "I tried to hang myself." Brenden wasn't so clear about why he was there. Something about a strange out-of-body experience and crossing paths with the police. Certified. We didn't talk much, simply sat there in silence together.

"Are you feeling anxious?" pressed a nurse as I recommenced my pacing. I didn't answer. Too caught up in my world of Voices and Plans, I practically ran up and down the halls. "Die, die, die! You messed up Our Plans but We will win! The girl, she dies!" I covered my ears, trying to shut Them out. "Bitch! Whore! You die tonight whether you want to or not. We will prevail!" *Noooo*, I cried. *Please, leave me alone.* Brenden came out of his room at the end of the corridor as I approached.

"Are you okay, Erin?"

"Bad night, bad night, really bad night." I clawed at my ears. "Bad bad bad bad bad," chorused the Voices. I couldn't even connect to Brenden as the Voices drew me into Their world. "It's bad."

I don't remember, but, seeing as nurses almost invariably react to anything remotely like anxiety (i.e., my pacing) with a PRN ("pro re nata" or "as needed" dose) of the sedative Ativan, I was most likely given one of those little pills. Which would mean that I was soon groggily in bed, sleeping the anxiety of the day away.

*　*　*

Thus my time on Laurel began. I was assigned to Dr. Surim for my psychiatrist, my first guide into the world of psychiatry. I did not connect with her at all. Looking back over the dozens of psychiatrists I've seen, she was one of the worst. She pounced on a diagnosis after the most cursory examination of my symptoms, making the erroneous assumption that since I had tried to kill myself I was depressed. But then, I didn't have any of depression's hallmark symptoms of change in appetite, sleep, or concentration, so she dropped me into the waste-basket diagnosis of dysthymia. That is, a little depressed, most of the time. *Diagnosis, done. Prescription? Celexa, an antidepressant. Any questions? No? Good. Our ten minutes are up.*

This was my first encounter with psych wards and their overworked psychiatrists, so I didn't know that my treatment was, as I see in retrospect, inadequate. Within a couple days, they were letting me go off on passes to roam the grounds unsupervised; after a week, I was allowed day passes to class. I heard Voices nearly constantly, and was seeing people that I passed on the streets as if they were being decapitated or hung right before my eyes. I walked by their dead ghosts, seeing at once both the hallucinatory dead and the real alive person. "Death, death, everywhere, and not a drop to drink," chanted the Voices.

All this I was accustomed to. It was ordinary to me, something I assumed everyone experienced but no one talked about. I looked at people around me, all so seemingly fine. Why couldn't I handle the Voices and Deep Meaning Plans like they could? Why did I end up in the looney bin, if they could cope so well? It never really occurred to me that I was experiencing the world any

24

differently from them; I thought it was just that I was terrible at coping. I knew I was at the end of my rope – figuratively, as well as literally, I noted with irony – but I simply thought that everyone else had the same short rope.

Given this mindset, it is not surprising that I told Dr. Surim very little of what I later found out to be the most telling of my symptoms. Classic symptoms of schizophrenia, my eventual diagnosis, were to me normal ways of experiencing and coping with reality. Although I didn't think that others heard the Voices that spoke to me, I did think everyone heard some personal variation of the same. I also confused delusion with a special ability to see the Deep Meaning of things. I let Dr. Surim's diagnosis of dysthymia explain my "flat affect" and "blunted emotions" as signs of depression, not schizophrenia. Perhaps I was just scared of the whole experience – of the experiences of the last few years of my life – and desperately wanted them to be explained by something as familiar and treatable to my Prozac generation as depression.

Strange thing, though, was the fact that I was generally happy throughout the length of my hospitalization. As usual, the Voices had to some extent subsided after the crisis had passed and the world seemed less full of Deep Meaning and obscure plans. Being locked on a hospital ward wasn't great, but I did have some good times, especially as I got to know some of the other patients. I attempted to coax Ellen into chatting or going out for walks, and tried just as unsuccessfully to get Jay to quiet down a little. My heart went out to Susanna, an elderly lady whose severe Parkinson's had led her into the black world of depression. Brenden and I continued to speak worlds with silent eyes, yet feeling that indescribable certainty that we were forever locked into those different inner worlds.

This sanctuary from the outside world had one unexpected breach: one of my professors had been admitted to Laurel a week or so before I had. Later, I heard bits and pieces of how she, uncharacteristically, acted aggressively toward a fellow professor and consequently ended up in the NS. She remembered me, I was sure, and seemed to be avoiding me. She kept mostly to herself, reading mindless novels and smoking endless cigarettes to help the long hours of the long days go by. I sought her out. I wanted to talk with someone who was, like I hoped to be, an academic. Someone intelligent, educated.

"I chose to come here," she answered when I finally asked outright. "I realized that I needed a safe place, somewhere that I can concentrate on getting the...." She paused, searching for the right analogy for the mental and emotional angst within. "The screaming chickens. To deal with the screaming chickens."

Yes, I knew about screaming chickens. That expression stuck with me. Screaming chickens.

Ellen started opening up, and though she still had to be dragged to any activity other than sleeping, we were able to connect a little. I coached her into going on the swings on the grounds, but she pumped her legs mechanically, without pleasure. She ate her meals, but each one was prefaced with the weary sigh: "The meal's here. I guess I'll eat." Her devoted parents came faithfully every night, and they placed uneventful hands of Gin Rummy and Crazy Eights.

The only indication of will, of personal exercise of volition I found was in her tale of why she had been brought here. Apparently, she had believed that if she kept her eyes closed long enough, she would open them to find a great, exciting, and wonderful party for her. Guests would be cheering, cake and ice cream plentiful. She even smiled, recounting this belief – or was it a wish? But then her eyes lost the small spark that had appeared, and she again expressed only empty inertia. She could live here, in the NS, forever, she said.

On a closed psych ward of perhaps 15 or so patients, comic relief is very welcome. I remember one evening clearly. Joanne – my former professor – was cleaning the small kitchen area we patients used to make peanut butter and jam sandwiches and coffee (decaf – even the tea was decaf. Anything to keep us low and easy to care for.). Leftovers from supper that night were lidded Styrofoam cups of coleslaw. We kept them in the ice bucket that also kept our milk cold. Since it was just left to anybody's initiative to dump out the melted ice and put fresh in, such leftovers often became "floaters" bobbing in the water. Tense from screaming chickens, both Joanne and I were trying to ease some of the stress by cleaning. She picked up the ice-turned-water container, and lo, the coleslaw swam around. I guess it struck her funny. "Look, they're swimming!" she exclaimed, and burst into laughter. I guess it struck me funny, then, too.

"A bath for the coleslaw!" I added.

"Clean coleslaw, coming up!"

"Anyone ready for a swim? Yes, we have a winner. Coleslaw!" Incredibly corny and lame, but it just cracked us up. We laughed together, two kindred patients locked on the psych ward and defying the screaming chickens to take away the humour of absurd nothings. Before or since then, I've never laughed with such necessity. We overcame the screaming chickens that night, and with mere coleslaw and cold water. If we could do that, we would surely conquer all our screaming chickens in time. Right?

27

* * *

I asked Joanne about the screaming chickens once more after that. I was crying, and pleaded with her as with someone who knew the pain of screaming chickens. "Do they ever go away?" She was many years my senior; was there hope?

"Do what go away?"

"The screaming chickens."

"What are screaming chickens?" she asked.

"That's the term you used before," I said, confused.

"I've never heard of screaming chickens," she snapped harshly, and turned back into her room. Feeling betrayed, I also retreated to my room. She did know about the screaming chickens, I was sure. *Is that the only way to deal with them?* I thought. *Would they never really be gone, only denied?*

* * *

I spent ten days on Laurel. Released, I felt empty and worthless, numb, nothing, without purpose, and guilty. I did what I always did: study. It was a coping mechanism, distracting me from the inner world. Now it was also a distraction from the burden of carrying a psychiatric diagnosis and its accompanying little pills. Although I had only spent just over a week in the NS, it was strange to be back in the "real world."

I was in my final year of a Bachelor's degree and I quickly caught up in my classes. I had begun my studies – with a handsome scholarship after having graduated second in my class at my high school with a 97% average in my hometown of Sackville, New Brunswick – at Mount Saint Vincent University (MSVU) in Halifax, Nova Scotia. Since I adored working with children, I enrolled in a degree in Developmental Psychology. I was happy enough and

28

sincerely loved the academics of term papers and exams. Third year, though, I took *Introduction to Neuroscience* as an elective and fell in love.

The brain fascinated me and I soon decided to switch my major. Being a small, undergraduate university, MSVU had little more to offer in the realm of Neuroscience, so I transferred to a Joint Honours BSc in Biology, with a minor in Chemistry, between MSVU and the larger Dalhousie University ("Dal"). I took my general classes, such as *Intro to Chemistry* and *Physiology*, at MSVU where class sizes were small, and the teachers more dedicated, and attended the advanced courses such as *Neuropsychiatry* and *Neuroscience Lab Techniques* at Dal. It was the best of both worlds.

Now I had to go talk with each of my professors. All were understanding and gave me flexibility in my missed assignments and tests. I didn't tell that what had transpired; I just handed over my excuse note from the hospital. To me, though, the NS letterhead screamed *crazy*.

Chapter 2: Schizophrenia, Developed and Defined

I never thought that I would end up in hospital again. I thought that it would just be that one time, that I had "hit bottom" and that things would change. But hitting bottom, I have come to realize, does not mean that you will bounce magically away from that low place, never to return. Spending time in hospital does not mean that you get cured. A drug may not work. But I had believed in a swift and complete recovery, and it shattered my sense of security to see myself back in hospital not a month later.

Relapse is very common in schizophrenia, the diagnosis I received during my second stay at the NS. Often, as I later came to find out myself, it is due to "medication noncompliance" (i.e., you don't take your meds) and that necessitates rehospitalization. Medication type or dose is then adjusted until the patient has gained enough insight to know when, how, and why such medication must be taken. A focus on anti-psychotic medication is backed by much data while other treatments such as psychotherapy ("talk therapy") alone do little for the patient suffering from schizophrenia. Medication noncompliance may stem from a variety of reasons; commonly, and in my case, the Voices demand it.

Such "Voices" are a cardinal symptom of schizophrenia, a form of auditory hallucination that plagues many schizophrenics. Hallucinations (which may also be visual or tactile), along with delusions (firmly-held convictions that are contrary to reality), form the diagnostic backbone of schizophrenia's "positive" symptoms ("positive" being those symptoms that are above and beyond normal experience; "negative" symptoms are a lack of something most people experience). Also included in the DSM-IV (Diagnostic and Statistical Manual, 4th Edition, the book used by professionals to diagnose psychiatric disorders) for the diagnosis of schizophrenia are paranoia and cognitive deficits or disorganization in which the patient loses track of conversations and may flit from topic to topic incoherently. It also somehow hijacks the cognitive function of "meaningfulness" thus letting the schizophrenic's delusions and hallucinations dictate what feels real to them. For me, I thought that the Deep Meaning was the fullness of insight and believed in it despite my neuroscientific education that would rationally tell me otherwise.

In addition to my positive symptoms, I also was plagued by schizophrenia's negative ones. I was extremely apathetic, my emotions blunted ("flat affect,") and spoke only with great effort ("poverty of speech"). I was asocial and did not care for relationships; pleasure eluded me ("anhedonia"). Memory loss was prominent for me, as it is for many. Unfortunately, the vast majority of anti-psychotic medications do not deal with these negative symptoms and social, vocational, and emotional disabilities remain.

Schizophrenia affects around one percent of the population worldwide. Typically, it develops in adolescence or early adulthood (usually somewhat later for females; I was "textbook" in that I was first diagnosed at age 22). There is often a genetic component, but not always (so lucky me, out of the genetic blue – I have no known schizophrenia in my family). For some reason, there are more winter babies with schizophrenia than those born in other seasons (and I am a February baby). It is one of the most costly diseases, amounting to $2.3 billion in Canada in 2010. This cost includes the frequent, often lengthy, hospitalizations of, and the expensive medicines prescribed for, patients suffering from schizophrenia.

Drugs for the treatment of schizophrenia first appeared in the mid-1900s and include the well-used and well-known Haldol (generic name haloperidol) and Largactil (chlorpromazine). These potent anti-psychotics have significant side-effects including involuntary, repetitive, and permanent movements called tardive dyskinesias and extrapyramidal symptoms (EPS) that include, ironically, the inability to initiate or cease movements. Additionally, EPS may manifest as symptoms that resemble Parkinson's disease (such as tremor and rigidity). They are now only used when several other (newer) medications have been tried without successful remission of symptoms (as was my case at one point in my anti-psychotic medication career). They do little in the treatment of negative symptoms. In later years, however, "second-generation" or "atypical" anti-psychotics have come to be widely used. Risperidone, olanzapine, clozapine, quetiapine, ziprasidone, aripiprazole, and others (most of which I have tried over the years) have fewer side-effects and may address negative symptoms.

As a neuroscientist, I know that, without medication, the activity in my brain is, to put it simply, characterized by too much dopaminergic activity. Dopamine is a neurotransmitter, a molecule that sends information from neuron to neuron in certain circuits of the brain. Anti-psychotics reduce the amount of dopaminergic activity, thus alleviating the symptoms of schizophrenia. However, there are also other circuits using different neurotransmitters such as serotonin and noradrenaline that are also affected in schizophrenia. The newer, second-generation anti-psychotics influence these other neural systems, providing some relief of negative symptoms that is not achieved by the older drugs. I have personally experienced the effects of these medications and am very thankful that "mere" pills can change so much.

The chapters to come detail my many hospitalizations and drug trials so typical of a young woman suffering from schizophrenia. I understand it from both outside and within: the neuroscientist in me thinks of dopamine and pharmacology while I, the patient, long simply for the quietness of no Voices, delusions, paranoia, and negative symptoms. I have had highs and lows; I have preferred one drug over another and been either heard or ignored by the professionals who have dealt with me. (Some of their chart notes have been quoted in this memoir.) I have learned that medicated Erin is very different from non-medicated Erin, and have then wondered who I "really" am. I write to give you, the reader, insight into my two worlds.

Chapter 3: Telling

I had a sense of things being ethereal, like I was in a dream. There were again the ghostly visions of people being decapitated or hung as I passed them on the street, which did little to ground me in reality. However, I had gained the insight that the suicidality that I had experienced was not typical. I had, ironically, learnt this in talking with the other patients on the crazies ward; surely, I thought, if people there hadn't all been through such, then it must be even more unlikely that the average person "on the outside" would have experienced it.

I felt compelled, driven to talking about what I had gone through and asking others if they knew – from experience – these things. I really had no sense of propriety about it, no internal check saying, *These things are private.* It must have been quite a shock to some of those I told. I focused on the suicidality. Having been diagnosed as dysthymic, and having been prescribed an antidepressant, I didn't yet realize that the root of the suicidality was a response to my schizophrenia and not to depression. Symptoms of delusion (the Deep Meaning) and hallucination (the Voices) still seemed to me normal human experience and so I didn't talk about them, just like we don't talk about how, exactly, music moves us to dance.

I remember, in hindsight, how I shocked some people. The stereotype of someone who has been to the NS is that they had a so-called nervous breakdown. Someone depressed or manic or anxious. That much can be said appropriately, but the details are to be left unsaid. I, still encumbered with a schizophrenic's lack of insight into socially-prescribed rules, talked about the hanging itself.

"I never would have thought you would be someone who would... do that," Crystal, the technician at the lab in which I was doing my Honours thesis, said after I told her what had happened. She was visibly upset. "I can't imagine if you hadn't... if you...." She couldn't finish her sentences. At the time, it didn't really bother me. Suicidal thoughts and gestures were to me commonplace. However, by beginning to talk about my experience I began to realize that I might have more problems needing psychiatric intervention than I had until then thought.

Soon after my return to the lab, my supervisor drew me aside. "Are you doing okay, Erin?" Thousands of thoughts and images flew through my mind. Okay? What did that mean? My mouth opened and my story poured out. I don't remember the words I used, but I vividly remember his face. There was shock, lightly covered with disbelief. Varnished, as it were, on top was an attempt to hide these first reactions with a socially-correct distant sympathy. "Well, if you ever need to talk, Erin..." he said. But with what was, for me, savant-like insight, I now knew that Dr. Mason was that: a doctor, my supervisor, not a confidant or healer. Now feeling uncomfortable, I closed up and we left that little room.

*　　*　　*

Dr. Uxyar was in her office. Nervously, I crept

around the corner and into her field of view. "Hi," I said. She looked up.

"Erin! Come on in." Mirroring her enthusiasm with shyness, I slid into a chair. Dr. Uxyar and I had struck up a sort of friendship that term, after my taking her Neuropsychiatry courses at Dal and excelling in them. I liked her bold, sure ways: no pretence, no chit-chat. She was warm and inviting, neither pushy nor reticent.

"I guess you know," I began, "that I couldn't make it to the exam." I was referring to the exam I had been supposed to proctor the week before. She nodded, waiting. "Well, I ended up in the hospital."

"Oh! What hap – I mean, sorry, you don't have to tell me what happened, if you don't want to. But are you okay now?"

"It was… well, they put me on medication. I was there ten days, though." She was silent, watching me. She didn't invite me to share, but her quiet attention seemed to spur me on to talk. "It was the NS," I continued. Still, the silence. It was supportive, without pressuring me to either speak or to remain silent. "They called me dysthymic. Put me on antidepressants." I waited a moment, remembering Dr. Mason's reactions. "For attempted suicide."

Finally, a response. "Oh, Erin." Tears in her eyes.

"Yeah. I tried to hang myself. I… well, it….." I had no more words. My confession hung there between us.

Did she talk then? Or did I keep babbling? The actual words and silences escape me now, but the care she extended remains clear in my memory. That day began a new type of friendship between us. I would confide in her many times, she would convey a sense of motherly caring; we would talk, and then email when I moved away. I still can't quite pinpoint what it was that drew me to her, but I like to believe that there was something unique in our relationship, and that she felt it, too.

How long did I spend there in Dr. Uxyar's office that day? I had an appointment with Patti, and that promted me to leave. I walked over to Psychological Services, mentally and emotionally undone. It was, however, a positive undoing, one that made me feel connected and ready to battle the demons within.

"Yes, I'm supposed to see Patti at 3:30," I told the receptionist. It had been the one condition on my release from the NS: I had to "see someone" on a regular basis. Patti was the first of many to treat me over the years, although, since Patti couldn't prescribe my medication, I also had an outpatient psychiatrist at the NS. I wonder now when it was that I became used to the idea that I would always be in the care of a professional.

"Come on in, Erin." I entered, anxious.

"So a lot has happened since I last saw you," Patti began. I looked around her room, unsure of where to begin. I tried to anchor myself, examining her lush plants, the tissue box (was I supposed to cry?), the view out the windows to the student-filled campus below. "Tell me about your time in the NS," Patti tried again.

This more direct prompt gave me a starting point. "I was there ten days," I began. "I talked with the other patients. And to people after I was released. A lot of stuff that I thought was common experience isn't. I never knew that most people don't try to kill themselves, or even think about it."

Patti was quiet, waiting for more. "I've finally come to the point where I realize that I need help. For me, being admitted to the NS was a final breaking point. It was a very concrete message to me that I couldn't fix myself. Here

37

were psychiatrists – experts, authorities, to me – passing the judgement that I needed to be there. It was a kind of relief, I think, that I didn't have to figure out whether I needed psychiatric help or not. They made that decision for me. I could argue with myself forever, strive to be the best student, try to convince myself that I can handle things, but here was a prescribed escape from that fruitless and sometimes devastating self-delusion." I silenced, spent. I rarely used so many words at once in this context of reflection and self-expression. It was as if I was beginning a process of rebirth and, like a preschool child, language flowed while I looked to others intently in an attempt to know myself through their reactions.

"You've shared a lot, Erin," Patti said. "What we need to do now is figure out how we are going to make sure that something like this doesn't repeat itself. We need a contract of how you are going to keep yourself safe."

"I've 'hit bottom,' as they say. I won't end up at that point again."

"I'd like to believe that, Erin, but we don't have such guarantees in life. In fact, you are, statistically, more at risk of future suicide attempts. The best I can do for you is to help you gain insight and learn to make better responses to the things in life that put you at risk of harming yourself."

"So what do I do?"

"I'd like to make a verbal contract with you. I know that a promise can't really stop you from hurting yourself, but such an agreement does help many patients. It becomes like a check: when you start to feel suicidal, this objective fact – 'I made a promise' – can help you stop, even though you may not, in the moment, understand why you shouldn't hurt yourself. It doesn't help you with the underlying reasons, but it may help keep you alive long enough to work through them."

"Sounds okay." It did make sense. I was glad that it should be seen as objective. Emotional promises may seem binding in the present, but when the feeling fades and hallucinations and delusions overwhelm, I am very vulnerable. Perhaps an objective command to myself could penetrate my schizophrenic mind effectively.

Patti and I therefore worked not on figuring out the main *issues*, but on the exact wording of a statement that I would be able to bring to mind in a crisis situation. "Like I said," Patti reminded me, "as long as you are kept safe, we will have all the time you need to work through the reasons and emotions behind this suicide attempt."

Patti had me repeat the contract a couple of times before leaving: *I will not try to kill myself without calling someone*. On a certain level, the promise seemed to say that I could commit suicide as long as I told someone first (I could certainly get it done before they could get to me). Yet for me at that point, it meant that I would reach out to someone, thereby anchoring myself in the reality that does not want me dead. Patti then had me make a list of the people I could call in such a situation. If the first person I called wasn't there, I was to keep calling down the list until I reached someone. *I will not try to kill myself without calling someone.* Would it really help?

Chapter 4: The NS Again

I am a person of my word. This integrity, as well as the specific and objective nature of the contract, kept me in line. I was determined to rise up from the "bottom" I had "hit."

"Yeah? Well, fuck you, girl. You know Our Reality is so much more important than anything a silly mouse-counsellor says. You die, girl. Die! Let her hang!" They followed me relentlessly. I still thought that I had had a magical experience by being admitted to the NS: I would now be strong enough to triumph over the Voices and Their Plans. Judging from Their unchanged harassment, though, it seemed that They believed that They would still win. I looked around at all my fellow students on campus and wondered, baffled and in some sort of awe, how they managed to function so normally. How did they resist their Voices and thwart Their Plans alone, when I could barely control Them even when hospitalized or in therapy?

I continued to live a mostly isolated existence. My apartment was my haven, but also my battleground: I was relieved of the necessity of putting on the front that I had it all together, but I also had fewer cues to ground me in reality. At home, alone, the Voices dominated. They tempted me repeatedly, angry that I was sticking by my promise to Patti and to myself. "Come on, it's here. Girl-bitch, come die," They would begin, almost nicely.

I will not try to kill myself without calling someone. My mantra.

"Fuck it, bitch." Did They go on to inform me of Their Plans and the Meanings behind them through auditory hallucination, or did They communicate via thought-waves? Somehow, I just knew, knew that there were Meanings everywhere and Plans in place. Electrical cords were nooses waiting to be tied, pills magical candies that would send me to the world of the Deep Meaning.

"Hi. Yaliel?"

"Hi Erin. How's it going?" *How is it going? I'm calling to keep from killing myself, that's how it's going.*

"Oh, okay," I answered vaguely. We chatted a few minutes, but then he had to go.

"See you at the lab, Erin." Abruptly I lost my connection to the real world. However, it was enough to keep me safe and I managed to keep to my contract the rest of the week. I called people sometimes – a feat in itself for me, given the pressure of the Voices and delusions telling me that calling other people was evil narcissism. I never let on to the people I phoned the real reason for the call. I was at least able to report back to Patti the next week. *I can do this,* I thought.

At this time, I was also drawing a lot of support from Dr. Uxyar. Her door was always open for me, and she seemed to brighten up when she saw me. I helped her out with a few things – some marking, some photocopying, some proctoring – thankful for the distraction and contact.

At one point she thought it made sense to give me the key to one of her student rooms, so I would have some of my own space in which to work. It quickly became a shelter for me, and I would sleep curled up on the floor. After one such nap, I looked up at the chair from my position on the floor. It had one of those back supports on it, with the strap that held it in place hanging invitingly loose and long. It was a cue.

I didn't promise anything about things that were set up for me, I thought. *Here it is, a prepared invitation for my responsibility.* I quietly looped the strap around my neck and lay back down on my stomach. The pressure of the strap-noose was inexplicably soothing.

"That's it, Erin. Quietly, peacefully. Dying girl," the Voices offered, confirming my feelings of the presence of the Deep Meaning. I relaxed in the noose.

Clip, clip, clip, clip. Footsteps – someone was coming! What if it was Dr. Uxyar or another one of her students who had a key to the room? No one must know about this, especially at this precarious point of being on the verge of completing the suicide for the Deep Meaning. If anyone saw, the Voices would torment me for it. It had to be done in total privacy; exposure would nullify my sacrifice to the Voices and their Plans. Quick – out of the noose, off the floor, hide the marks the strap had imprinted on my neck under my turtle-neck sweater. Evidence gone, I sat at the desk with a textbook open in front of me. Clip, clip, clip.... The footsteps approached, and then faded as they passed my room and continued down the hallway. False alarm, I thought at first. "No, just a test," a male Voice informed me.

This "test" sort of backfired on the Voices, though, as it had gotten me out of the noose. I left the room. When I

42

told Dr. Uxyar, she took my key. I figured that to mean that the strap-noose was not what the Deep Meaning had prepared for me. So I waited.

*   *   *

I was looking for a quiet place to eat my lunch and look over my class notes when I found the set-up prepared for me. It was on the sixth floor of the Biology building. Against large windows that gave a beautiful view of the trees bathed in their fall colours, with the vast Atlantic Ocean in the distance behind them, it wasn't what I'd expected. There was a table and a couple of indoor plants, giving the corner a peaceful quality. It was isolated, too: no one was around. I sat down at one end of the table and took out my lunch and books.

It was then that I noticed the noose. Two holes had been drilled through the table at the end I had just "happened" to have sat down at, and a strong plastic-covered wire had been looped through. At the time, I did not jump to the logical conclusion that it was there perhaps to secure expensive equipment against theft. To me, it was clearly a case of a set-up by the Plans of the Deep Meaning.

I glanced up, nervous. *This is it*, I thought. A sign then caught my eye: "Overcoming Procrastination." There it was! The final sign – a sign. *How clever*, I thought, smiling. I read the sign again. Ah, it was disguised as an announcement for a course at Counselling Services, so no one else would realize its true intent. But I, I was given the insight of the Deep Meaning.

"She's Overcoming Procrastination," a chorus of Voices proclaimed. Indeed I was. The wire was around my neck. I lay my head down on my folded arms, hiding it underneath my sweater's collar. "It looks like she's sleeping. Aw, cute," the Voices commented. "And see, she's

43

pulling the wire tightly from under the table. Discreet. Yay, Erin, you got it! Dying girl, girl dying."

Tighter, tighter I pulled. Now I could reach the lower loop with my foot, which was better because before when I fainted my grasp on the wire would slacken and the critical strangulation would not occur. The dead weight of my leg should be sufficiently heavy, though. How rational I was in the midst of this irrational act.

Clip, clip, clip, clip. Again, footsteps. *This will be the test*, I thought. They passed by, seeing only a sleepy student laying her head on the table for a quick nap between classes. Nothing of note, nothing out of the ordinary. I could hear applause in the distance, the Voices were so pleased. People couldn't see what was going on; therefore, I reasoned with schizophrenic reason, it wasn't really killing myself. I didn't feel that I was breaking the contract with Patti. This had been so Predestined for me, so Right. The sign was there, the method prepared, all without letting anyone know. Perfect.

Perfect, except that it didn't work. Everything went black, but then my foot must have slipped out of the loop, because next thing I knew I was opening my eyes and looking out the window. What had happened? My neck was sore. A wire? Suddenly, I remembered. Suicide? But I didn't want to die. What were They doing to me? I had to get away. My fingers pulled at the wire. So tight, hard to loosen. Footsteps again! Quick, hide the noose, pretend you're sleeping. Okay, they're gone. Untie it! There, now slip my head out. Ooh, sore. Free, I sit up. What now?

I headed straight for the SUB, up the stairs. Same kind receptionist, another emergency appointment. Patti, asking if I could wait until four. Yes, I'll be okay. Down to the second floor to wait out the hour and a half. I was in another world. I slumped against the wall, spent. I reached for a pencil and paper, hoping that journalling would help me sort it all out. I began writing, and I was back by the window, reliving the whole experience:

"What illogical mind convinces me so utterly, almost so fatally, that I am supposed to kill myself? Stupid, stupid – not rational, not right. Where does that voice go? I never break my promises but now I almost broke my life when I broke this one.... Faith – in Their plan; and a blind leap... this is your privilege your duty your right.... Finally, overcoming procrastination. A sign (a sign) just to reassure me that I am right in thinking that now I am supposed to really die.... Another vision: those gasps as I am flung out of my hanging head and I can see me – you – there. You are dying and out here I scream oh no oh no oh no. This is not supposed to be.... Die, die: you must.... Now here I am alive I think. No it didn't happen did it?... How do I stay not irrational? I have to tell. Have to. Have to. Another "supposed to" is this one right?"

* * *

Patti drove me over to the NS. She left me there, alone, until the nurse called me in to talk with the admitting psychiatrist. It was Dr. Salim. I quickly got the idea that she was annoyed to see me back. After all, hadn't she "fixed" me just a couple weeks ago?

"What did you do that for?" she fired at me after reading Patti's notes. Translation: stupid girl, why are you bothering me? I cringed, folding myself almost double in the chair. "Well?" By then I was rocking myself back and forth, back and forth, desperate. More words hurled at me, and I lost track of whether it was Dr. Salim or the Voices or even me. I was shutting down. I couldn't take so many harsh Voices drowning me in Their intensity, Their insistence, Their insensitivity.

Insanity.

That is, Dr. Salim certified me. I had refused to be admitted voluntarily, refused to be locked up and medicated. It hadn't worked before, so why think that I would get any real help this time? "Will you just admit yourself, Erin, and get it over with," Dr. Salim said impatiently. More harsh tones to echo my Voices.

"Noooo, no," was all I could get out. "No, please, no. Not the hospital again."

I was ushered up to Mayflower unit. No Short Stay this time; they knew I was sicker than that. Here's your room, your hospital blues – you don't have any clothing privileges yet – and here's some Ativan to settle you down.

I wandered, over to the locked ward door: I could see across to Laurel, the ward I had been on before. I waited, glimpsing Susanna, then Ellen. Brenden. I wondered about Jay. "Get away from the door," a nurse commanded impatiently. Slowly I left it, drifted into the common area. Sitting on the couch, I was soon joined by curious patients. A sweet young guy – 18 maybe? – with red, red hair. Why was I in there? Anorexia? he guessed. That surprised me, flattered me. I had weighed in at 118 pounds at admission, which was fat for me. He hugged me, but I felt no comfort, nothing but dissociation.

"No, I tried to hang myself," I answered blandly and walked away. Certified. The Voices were so loud and consistent I could almost ignore Them. They weren't saying anything I hadn't heard a thousand times before.

When I had been on Laurel, I had thought that Mayflower, as seen through the door windows, was crazier. *Hopefully more interesting, now that I am locked up over here*, I thought. At least one thing would be much better, I realized: Dr. Salim worked on Laurel. I'd be getting a new psychiatrist, and virtually anyone would be better than her. However, today was Friday, and my psychiatrist didn't come in Fridays, instead working late the other four days of the week. So to just tide me over until Monday, Dr. Jeshel had a nurse usher me in to talk with him.

I was feeling better than last night, assuming that I would only be in another ten days or so. I talked freely, explaining and describing what had led up to this hospitalization. He was interested in details and soon had me describing the incident at Dal.

"I saw a sign saying "Overcoming Procrastination" and knew that the Time had come," I explained. "And it was all ready – the wire, the sign, the place. It was perfect, so Right, so in tune with the Deep Meaning," I went on. "And the peace when I tightened the noose. It was so perfect. They prepared everything so perfectly for me." I smiled, flooded again with that profound sense of Rightness and Obedience.

"You find this funny?" Dr. Jeshel demanded. His mean eyes leered at me from their little slits in his fat, puffy face. His bald head glistened with sweat. I was supposed to communicate to this man the fathomless joys of the Plan?

"No, not funny," I replied. Perfect. Right. Joy and peace and contentment, the fulfilling of destiny. The Deepest Meaning – and I had been granted access into it! But I left these unsaid. He was not worthy of Revelation.

Monday I met my new psychiatrist. Dr. Kate Giffin was petite and professional in her slim navy skirt and heels. Clip, clip, clip. She walked so fast, a rabbit compared to the medicated turtles meandering the halls. She was accompanied by a psych resident, Dr. Anderson (but call me Brent, smile). Question time.

I didn't quite "click" with this clippity psychiatrist

on a personal level, but I sensed that she was "good" and even someone "good" for me. Her questions probed for reasons, not just a cataloguing of my symptoms. I don't remember which session, but I do know that it was early on in my stay on Mayflower that she began to get me talking about the Voices and Their Plans. With that, she became the first professional to suggest that what I suffered from was schizophrenia. Although she was careful not to give me such a diagnosis quickly, it always hovered in the background. Officially, I had "psychosis, not otherwise specified." A throw-away diagnosis, really, since my psychosis was actually just a symptom of my schizophrenia, and not the full disorder, just as having a sore throat is only a symptom of having a cold.

Dr. Giffin took me off the antidepressant, Celexa, and started me on risperidone (Risperdal). This was to be my first of eight anti-psychotic drugs that I would try over the next eight years. "Every person's brain chemistry is different" is the adage in medication-focused psychiatry. So while many people respond well to risperidone, I did not. Instead, I began developing symptoms of parkinsonism. This stiffness, slowness of movement, tremors, and "masked face" are are common side-effects of many anti-psychotics and relate to dopamine. In Parkinson's disease, a certain part of the brain in which dopamine is used degenerates, manifesting as motor dysfunction. (Its medical treatment is drugs that enhance dopaminergic activity.) When anti-psychotics dampen the effects of dopamine, the side-effect of parkinsonism may occur.

I also began to develop akathisia. "The walkies" some call them, but this name does little justice to what can only be called pain. It was as if all my motor neurons were firing wildly for my legs, arms, and torso to move, but no matter how much I exercised them I couldn't relieve the intense desire to MOVE. The neuroscience behind akathisia is poorly understood, but some medications, such as propranolol, clonazepam, and benztropine, often offer some respite. For me, propranolol was moderately effective.

Soon, I was lucky to have grounds privileges. The NS was built on a large tract of land beside the Atlantic Ocean offering seaside and treed trails I could walk and walk and walk for my akathisia. The hospital had opened its doors in 1858 as the Mount Hope Asylum for the Insane. Ironically, it was founded by Hugh Bell, whose award I would win for being the most promising Biology researcher of my Honours class.

In addition to the quiet paths, there was a swing-set, which I loved. I swung high; the rhythm calmed me, as did the waves of the sea. I looked out to where the sea met the sky and yearned for a life free of the things I was learning were not ordinary but from illness.

Inside, Dr. Giffin was uncovering my secret Voices and Plans. When I was questioned about my psychotic symptoms, I became distressed, defensive, hiding my face and continuously rocking in my chair. She was building up a diagnosis: schizophrenia, paranoid type, while I began to realize that so much of what I thought was normal was in fact schizophrenic.

I looked backwards to my childhood, both with Dr. Giffin and by myself. My first few memories of auditory hallucination weren't like the later, abusive Voices. I remember car rides in particular:

The music played quietly in the background. Clear, soft classical sounds drifted out of the car's trunk and enveloped me in their peaceful tones. I loved these concerts, but they were sometimes hard to hear. "Mommy, can you please turn up the music?" my five-year-old voice asked politely.

"What music, Erin? The radio's not on," answered my mother.

"Oh," I said, and went back to enjoying my concert. How could I have known that these wonderful songs were not sung for everyone? I just sat back and strained my ears for the comforting music while my parents talked quietly in the front seats and my three-year-old sister, Kyla, slept soundly beside me.

*   *   *

The auditory hallucinations followed me to elementary school. There, too, They were pleasant enough and did not disturb me:

For two days, we had no school. The blizzard brought a couple of feet of snow and the snowplows piled it high in the school parking lot. The high hills of snow reminded me of ragged cliffs and mountains, and I transformed into an agile mountain goat.

"Look at her, so sure-footed. Just like a mountain goat."

How had she (the Voice was female) known that I was pretending to be a mountain goat? I peered over the other side of the snow pile but saw no one that matched the Voice.

"Look at her jumping from mountain top to mountain top," I heard as I leaped around. "So sure-footed. Yes, sure-footed." The Voice added. It was using a word I had just learned a few weeks ago. Sure-footed. Yes, I was sure-footed, I thought. I looked around again to see who had given me the compliment. My sister's first-grade teacher was nearby, but it did not sound like her. Then there were the children, many of them playing on the drifts and banks. But it had been an adult voice, I was sure.

I was confused. Who was talking about me? "Hello Jello, sure-footed, that mountain-goat girl. Look at her!"

Who wanted people to look at me? I was shy – I hated being the centre of attention – and here there was someone hiding

50

and drawing attention to me! But as I looked around, the other children were paying me no special attention. Surely they heard the Voice; It was so loud. Finally, I stopped trying to make sense of It and simply revelled in Its compliments. I was sure-footed, and proud of it.

* * *

I remember third-grade recesses very clearly. I was a loner, by choice. I happily watched the other girls run off to play their communal games while I retreated to my favourite spot: an inward corner. It was quiet there and I was free to think or talk with my Voices.

In those days, the Voices spoke so sweetly. They encouraged me, complimented me, taught me Their Wisdom. I listened with rapt attention, answering aloud or in my head; They could understand either mode of communication. I still wasn't sure what or who They were, but I at least knew that They were trustworthy and good.

"You are different from the other children," They told me. "Special. Chosen. Stay with Us and good things will happen. But," They added, the first shadows of the menace to come, "know that bad things will happen if you disobey Us."

I was happy to obey. I was, on the whole, a very obedient girl to my parents and teachers, so it was no big deal to submit to these body less adults. I played with Them faithfully every recess and in return They gave me a sort of security and friendship. "Friend Erin, be Our friend, no end, never lend, always bend," They'd say. For some reason, they liked to speak in rhymes.

* * *

Another of Their favourite practices was to comment on what I was doing and who I was, and to pass Their all-knowing judgement. This is a common and classic symptom of schizophrenia. "Alone with Us, good. Look at the good girl! She listens to Us, right-o, listen glisten to us

51

on a bus. She stands so still and quiet. We like her. She is good, very good should."

How was I to know that these benign hallucinations were precursors to the malignant, dark, and destructive ones I would experience later in life? As They didn't cause me any real difficulties, I gave Them little thought and took Them for granted. No one thought to ask, either. I was just a quiet, extremely shy, little girl; I excelled at school and gave very little trouble at home. I played with friends – not many, and certainly not the popular ones, but a few close ones. I loved to read.

It was only as I grew older that my freedom became more restricted by the Voices. They slowly grew less gentle or nice and became harsh, judgemental, and downright *mean*. "Stupid girl! Don't do that! Do that and we punish you!"

Their two favourite things to punish were buying things and talking to people. I quaked at the thought of purchasing something as little as a chocolate bar or a coffee. It simply wasn't worth the onslaught of harsh, condemning Voices. My "shyness" persisted as I tried to handle the Voices that seemed just as real as a person talking to me. Still, I didn't tell anyone about them. I feared scorn and ridicule: everyone else could manage their internal struggles. Was it not as hard for them? Was there some developmental ease that I missed and had to create? So I worked harder, and kept, outwardly, my excuse of shyness. The schizophrenia was emerging, but no one – myself included – knew what was happening.

* * *

When I entered the hospital, I was clearly showing signs of schizophrenia. I was writing a lot, but my charts called these papers "pseudophilosophical" and "bizarre." I had what are called "ideas of reference:" I thought people could read my mind. As the risperidone started to work, many of my symptoms eased or abated. Only by their absence did I come to understand what was disease and what wasn't. I had been sceptical that any drug, let alone an anti-psychotic, could change me... but it did. It was the beginning of insight.

These unexpected results led me to wonder (rationally) that perhaps I did in fact have schizophrenia and was responsive to the pharmaceutical treatment. However, since I couldn't tolerate a therapeutic dose of the risperidone due to the parkinsonism, I was switched to another anti-psychotic medication: olanzapine (Zyprexa). It is very well known that olanzapine causes significant weight gain. It catches you both ways: it increases your appetite and slows down your metabolism. I began to gain weight and this terrified me. You see, I was bulimic.

Chapter 5: Bulimic, Guilty, and Naïve

It had started in July of 2001, the day after I moved to my first roommate-free apartment. I weighed myself that morning: 106 pounds. For five-foot-five me, it meant I was quite underweight. I was pleased, especially since I hadn't been watching my weight or trying to lose. My metabolism was youthfully high and the daily trek up the hills of MSVU kept me burning calories. I ate whatever I wanted, but my weight stayed low.

That day, I ate ice cream. A lot. Food comforted me, distracted me from the inner turmoil of my persistent, negative Voices. Finally, after eating almost the whole two-litre container, I felt extremely overstuffed and uncomfortable.

I then remembered that some people make themselves sick to empty their stomachs. While most bulimics do this to avoid weight gain, at the moment I just wanted physical relief. So I went into the bathroom, hunched myself over the white toilet, and pushed my finger down my throat. Instant success: I heaved, and the ice cream, still cold, came up and out.

The relief was immediate and intoxicating. It was a rush of adrenaline, a feeling of being completely cleansed inside. Like a potent drug, it got me hooked the very first time.

As soon as I realized that I could purge myself of anything I ate, I began binging. I was hurt, lonely, and sad, so I ate. Larger and larger binges, with more and more success in the purging after. However, my purging wasn't perfect yet, and I began to gain weight. By the second time I arrived at the NS that fall, I weighed 118 pounds. I felt huge.

Through my first hospitalization and into my second, I continued to binge and purge in the hospital. I strategically appointed myself Stacker of Trays. After each meal, I'd collect the used trays and stack them neatly for the kitchen worker who would retrieve them. This meant I could scavenge stray food, especially the many untouched desserts.

I ate a lot of rice pudding, which was good because I had by this point learned that some food came up more easily and more completely than others. Rice pudding was among the easy ones. The purging was a bit tricky, as the washrooms were right across from the nurses' station. So I developed a sneaky way: throw up into the shower drain. The running water masked the sounds of my retching and all the evidence drained away nicely. Still, with the combination of imperfect purging and the olanzapine, I was soon up to 123 pounds. As any bulimic can attest to, all I felt was FAT.

I quickly met the DSM-IV diagnostic criteria for bulimia nervosa. I was binging ("eating, in a discrete period of time, an amount of food that is definitely larger than most people would") and felt "a lack of control over this eating." My self-induced vomiting ("purging") was in part to lose weight, in part to feel better after binging. It was happening several times a day, much more than the required (i.e., for diagnostic purposes) frequency of twice a week, for three months. Finally, I was "unduly influenced by body shape and weight." It would be years before I was officially diagnosed and treated, over a decade before I'd shed the bulimia for good.

*　*　*

A perhaps good thing was that Jay was back in the NS too, and on Mayflower. This was his 33rd admittance even though he was only in his early 30's. He was still as manic as ever, talking forever and quite interested in me. He had but one complaint: the tights I wore under my jumpers.

Apparently, every time I yanked at my tights to pull them up he got aroused. "Erin, stop it!" he exclaimed one day.

"What?" I asked, puzzled.

"Your tights – the way you keep pulling at them... it...," he trailed off, then began again. "When you do... that... it makes me, well, want you. You know? So please don't tease me with it anymore."

"I'm sorry," I said genuinely, having been truly unaware of this problem. "I'll be more discreet."

"In your room, or the bathroom, please, Erin."

"I'll try to remember. But it's so unconscious. Just remind me when I forget. Okay?"

"Yeah." He shrugged, looked at me, and walked back to his room. I felt bad. Poor guy getting mixed messages. At least I tended to remember the tights thing in the future.

One thing Jay convinced me of was the value of

attending occupational therapy, or OT. It was held twice a week, in the basement. While others sewed prefab leather pouches and painted terra cotta planters, I hid myself in the corner with children's paint and plenty of white paper. I had never painted artistically as an adult before, but this time, I didn't stop. Session after session, I painted out my feelings and thoughts in dramatic colours onto naïve whiteness. It was, indeed, therapy. In fact, the cover of this book is one of those paintings.

There were a few themes to my paintings, the most prominent one being the death of my grandfather. When I was 12 years old, and my younger sister, Kyla, only ten, Nana and Grampa, my Mom's parents, were visiting from Ontario to see their only and beloved grandchildren. I didn't know it at the time, but my Grampa was quite ill; he was emaciated and had a heart weakened by two previous heart attacks. All I, in my childish ignorance, knew, was that I was so happy to have them visit.

Then, it happened. It is morning and we are at our cabin, isolated on the cliffs of New Brunswick's East coast. I am just waking up in the loft where Kyla and I sleep when I hear a strange, loud noise. The rattle of death, I learned later, but at the time, I didn't know.

"Mark? Mark?!" I hear my father shout. I peek downstairs. There is Grampa, head bowed and body slumped at the dining table. "Mark!"

Now he is on the ground, Dad pumping frantically at his chest, trying to wrest the heart back into rhythm. Nana and Mom are there, Kyla and I. We have no phone. Grampa is dying. I see him. Blood trickles from his mouth onto his sweatshirt, staining it.

Dad races to the car to drive the few kilometres from our cabin to the nearest village and returns an eternity later with a nurse. "Does anyone know how to do CPR?" she asks.

"Is that the thing they teach you in swimming lessons?" I ask timidly.

"What?"

I am silent.

Grampa is dead.

Finally, Mom remembers that there are children present. "Girls!" she instructs rapidly. "Go up the road and show the ambulance where to go. Hurry!" Kyla and I pull on our black rubber boots and, still pyjama-clad, race up the steep, unending road. I am crying, shaking, terrified.

The ambulance takes the body away.

He is gone.

It is my fault. I knew CPR. I knew that was what Grampa needed. But I was too scared. So it is my fault. He is dead and I am to blame.

That guilt wracked me for years. Every time we'd practice CPR at swimming or in gym class, I would break down in tears. One time, years later, I asked what to do if blood is coming out of their mouth. "It means it's too late," the instructor said. Oh.

Before I heard that and began to realize that no one would expect a 12-year-old child to perform CPR on her dying grandfather, I judged myself as profoundly guilty. I began trying to smother myself with my pillow at night: I didn't deserve air. I started to refuse myself food: I didn't deserve sustenance. I simply didn't deserve to live and later that year I tried to slash my wrists with a razor, my first suicide attempt. Since it was just a safety razor (I didn't know any better) the cuts were superficial and I just hid my band-aided wrists under long sleeves until they healed. No one ever knew. Yet still, I was guilty.

All these feelings came bleeding out onto the clean white paper at OT in the NS. The colours of guilt, the vivid memories, the staining blood... me, crying, alone. It was, as professed, therapeutic. I could bring all the pain up and out and leave it there, on the paper. It was safe, paralleling therapy sessions with Dr. Giffin. I was small and sad and scared. I cried sometimes, quietly, to myself in my art corner. I painted and painted until it was okay enough to stop and say, *I have spoken*. That was OT.

* * *

A new guy came in February of 2002 while I was in my third month at the NS. James was tall and cute, intense and interesting.

"Do you play chess?" he asked me one day, his second there.

"A little," I admitted. So we dragged out a chessboard and men from the OT closet and set up in the dining room. One game led to another and we found we were a perfect match: we took turns winning and losing. Along with chess, we began to talk.

He was my age, early twenties, but had already started a family with his now-ex-girlfriend. His girls were five and three and absolutely adorable. "Daddy!" they'd shout when they came, running down the hallway to fling themselves in his waiting arms. He'd scoop them up together, them squealing with pleasure and him laughing. What uncommon sounds to hear on the psych ward. Nurses would pass by smiling, and I realized, as I watched him play with them, talk to them, simply love them, that I was drawn to him for it.

Soon, James answered my unspoken attraction and asked for something more than chess. Since such is unacceptable on the ward, we'd take staggered passes and walk the beautiful, ocean-side, wooded grounds. He kissed me, once, then again, carefully and respectfully.

Back on the ward, Jay was onto us. He was angry and sad, having voiced feelings for me ages ago only to have me say quietly, firmly, *No*. So for him to see me say *Yes* to James filled him with jealousy. That's why, when he told me that James had a "Past" in crime – breaking and entering and burglary – I tossed it off as envy. I should have listened.

James left the hospital soon after I met him, moving to a transition house for troubled youths with no place to go. Nevertheless, he visited me faithfully every day. Once, he was hugging me in the hall on Mayflower he let a word slip: love. "I'm just showing how much I love you," he said quietly in my ear when I worriedly pulled from his embrace lest he be asked to leave. Love? It made me nervous.

I continued to meet up with him on passes but he began to be more distant. By this time, he'd told me the things Jay had mentioned. He came out to dinner one night when my parents were in town and I left feeling embarrassed. He had swaggered a boast that he would be a millionaire by the time he was forty, though had no real plans on how to exactly accomplish this. *Crime* flit through my mind, since I was beginning to have doubts about James.

* * *

My university adviser, Helen, told me of a competition. The Neuroscience Department at the University of Calgary in Alberta had put out that they were looking for ten graduating undergraduate students from across Canada to come explore their graduate Neuroscience program. Applicants were to submit a resume and an essay. Though I was still in the hospital, I completed the forms and attachments and sent it all in.

I gave little thought to it until an email came a few weeks later: I had been chosen! One of ten, out of the whole country! Very soon, all the nurses and patients knew. To me, though, it was more than just being elected; it meant I could still compete, and do well, in academia (albeit the academia of a student). One possible hitch: I was still in the NS and the week in Calgary was set for mid-March, only six weeks away. I was determined to go. I suppressed my symptoms as much as I could, the olanzapine making this possible. I "worked hard" on my "issues" and obeyed every rule. I took my passes to prove I could function "on the outside." I even let up on the binging and purging.

Five weeks and six days later, I was discharged. It had taken a fair bit of pleading and perfect behaviour, but they had let me go. I had spent a total of four months there on Mayflower and it felt so strange to be loose on the streets. Everything had an unreal quality, as if sprinkled with fog and fairy dust. I felt unmoored but relatively confident that I could navigate the road ahead. There was little time for reflection, though: I was to board a plane to Calgary the very next day. There was to be another girl, Julia, from Dal going too, so I hoped and hoped that my certifiable craziness was in check.

"Julia," I called when I spotted her at the airport.

"Hi, Erin," she said, smiling. She looked at my small blue bag. "You sure pack light."

"Thanks," I said, accepting it as a compliment.

"Are you as excited as I am?" Julia asked with enthusiasm. "I've never been on a plane before. And I heard that it's really cold there right now, like minus 30. But that it's a dry cold there, not wet like here."

"Um," I replied, but she kept going. It was innocent

chatter and didn't really bother me, but I was glad we were not sitting beside each other on the long flight there. She probably talked the ear off her seat mate while I read and slept. I looked out my window and again felt so strange to be in the "real world". I had been in the NS four full months; I was now officially, documentedly, *crazy*. Oh, the official terms were *schizophrenia*, *psychosis*, *paranoia*, and *delusion*, but I knew it was just code for *crazy*. I wondered what it would all mean as I eased (jumped?) back into a "normal" life.

*   *   *

Calgary was a blur of tours, meetings, and lectures. We saw amazing facilities and the latest million-dollar equipment, evidence of Alberta's generous funding. As an NSERC (a national-level science scholarship worth almost twenty thousand dollars a year for two years) recipient, I was told that Alberta Heritage would automatically top-up my award by $5,000 – a lot of money to a 22-year-old student. We met with researchers to discuss their work and our potential role there as graduate students. I spent time discussing how neurons find their targets as the brain develops, how connections between neurons change throughout life, and how walking is controlled by alternating neuronal activity in the spinal cord. So many exciting prospects!

Socially, I kept to myself on down times, although I remember going to have sushi downtown. We went by transit and Julia and the other girls ate dish after dish of sushi. I nibbled one to try, and that was enough. I didn't like it. But it all – the spontaneous decision to go downtown for sushi, the busing there and back, the choosing of a restaurant – made me feel so *normal*. A part of a social group. I hadn't felt that in a very long time, unless you count being locked up with other crazies.

*   *   *

Back in Halifax, James had finally moved to his own apartment and brought his girls home. I visited him. Soon, he wanted sex. I was scared and virginally innocent.

"No," I said. "I'm not ready."

"Please?" he'd beg.

"No." After that, I only saw him once more. I was at his apartment (filthy, messy, with cigarette ashes and butts, and beer bottles everywhere) while he had a few other people over, doing nothing.

"Do you wan to go for a walk?" he said to me. Had he read my discomfort?

"Sure."

"One thing. I have money in my account for rent tomorrow, but I can't access it until next week. Could you lend me the money and I'll write you a cheque?"

"Um, I guess." I tried to think it through, but trusting, naïve me just took him at his word. We had a nice walk to an ATM, and then parted ways, with a kiss, so I could catch the bus home.

"See you tomorrow," he said.

"Bye."

I never saw him, or his money, again. The bank returned the bad cheque and I was out a full month's rent. Luckily, I had some money in my savings and didn't have to tell anyone how gullible I'd been. I went by James's apartment building a few times, unsure of my intentions, but rang the bell. No answer, ever.

Chapter 6: From East-Coast NS To West-Coast Riverview

Spending four months in the NS meant I had to drop my courses at the universities. However, I did get to go to my last Honours class to present my thesis. I had done all the work the summer before and put it into presentation format in the early fall so all I had to do was rehearse it again. And who better than an audience of mental patients? About six of them listened patiently to my neuro-speak on the developmental expression of Hsp27 in the retina of the neonatal rat and applauded me enthusiastically. It is a warm memory. Then, on a pass, I presented it to my class. I was a certified, drugged *crazy* person, but managed to receive the class's highest award for my work, presentation, and potential (the Hugh Bell award: "most likely to succeed in science"). I also had the prestigious NSERC award, which I could take to any university I wanted for my Master's.

I had researched schools, then professors, looking for a good fit with lots of possibility, settling on the University of British Columbia (UBC) for their excellent program in Neuroscience and on Dr. Andrew Blythe for his work on neurodegenerative disease. We'd been emailing since the

spring and had set arrangements for the fall term. However, having had to drop my courses, I was short of graduating that spring. Eager for me to join his lab, Andrew hired me as a technician while I took transfer credits at UBC until I graduated with my BSc in Biology that fall of 2002. Yes, it took three universities and five years, but I did it.

For my Master's, I was to study the ALS (amyotrophic lateral sclerosis, or Lou Gehrig's disease) part of ALS-PDC (ALS-parkinsonian-dementia complex), a disease once very common in Guam and thought to be caused by the traditional ingestion of cycad seeds. (Cycad trees resemble palm trees, are tropical, and have large seeds that can be ground into flour, made into a dough, and baked.) We modelled the disease in mice, feeding them homemade cycad pellets made from scratch from cycad seeds shipped to us from Guam. Another new Master's student, Daniel, and I shared a group of mice, with him studying the parkinsonian aspect of ALS-PDC. It was very nice to be working with him and I fondly remember our "pellet parties" when we'd make flavoured cycad pellets for our mice to eat.

My move from one coast to the other had a little "detour:" China. China? Yes, my sister, Kyla, was spending a year as an exchange student in Shanghai, becoming fluent in Mandarin and absorbing a culture so different from our own. I admired her willingness to venture into such a foreign country, her outgoing nature that drew people of all backgrounds to her, and her confidence in herself that made these adventures and friendships meaningful and lasting. Even though she was two years younger, I looked up to her. I wanted some of her ease with people and in social settings, her ready smile and optimistic outlook. These so often eluded me, but recognizing them in her gave me hope that I might cultivate them in my own life.

We thought this would be an opportunity for me to see part of the most-populated country. To my frustration, it passed in a blur of olanzapine: eating and sleeping. I did meet her boyfriend, Simon, and liked him; luckily enough, as he has since become a beloved brother-in-law. As I write, they are expecting their first child.

*   *   *

Over the months of therapy I underwent in the hospital, I learned how to figure out what my symptoms (i.e., as opposed to normal human experiences) were: whatever the psychiatrists were most interested in. What they asked questions about. What they said would abate or at least lessen with medication. I learned their words: hallucination, delusion, paranoia, flat affect.

This education began in the NS and continued throughout my subsequent interactions with the mental health care system. At first, I couldn't make the proper distinctions; I thought everyone had their own Voices and suicidality. After all, didn't everyone at times talk about the "little voice" in their head? Or say, flippantly, when stressed over a mistake, *"Oh, I could just kill myself!"* I reasoned that they simply kept the depth and degree of their torment under wrap and functioned easily in social situations. I berated myself for not being able to silence my screaming chickens. I was, therefore, someone who kept to herself. Alone, I could yell back at the Voices and weep over Their Plans to have me kill myself.

In public, with friends or family, I was the quiet one. It was my best defence and charade as I tried to be like everyone else, to smile and talk and work. My schooling became my escape from the torment of the Voices and Their Plans and my success at university made everyone think that I was fine, normal. I threw myself into my classwork, earning a near-perfect GPA of 3.26 out of a possible 3.30: an A+ average during my undergraduate years in Halifax. Even while in the NS during the fall term, I did stellar work on my assignments, particularly in the Neuroscience classes I loved.

Still, I came off a bit odd, earning me a diagnosis of Asperger's syndrome by the psychologist at MSVU in Halifax. My long-time roommate agreed, citing my substantial social awkwardness, my innocent and literal acceptance of what others told me, and my sensitivity to social and sensory overload. That diagnosis, however, was left behind in Halifax and in Vancouver, it was all about the schizophrenia.

* * *

"Erin!" I heard my name and turned to see Auntie Cathy waving. Uncle John headed towards my luggage cart and a timid, 11-year-old Sarah hung back. Three-year-old Jillian, on the other hand, came forward. They had all come to meet me at the airport in Vancouver upon arrival from China.

"Did you come on a big, big plane, Ewin? Did you?" Jillian asked immediately. She, certainly, was not shy. She babbled happily as my bags were put in the trunk and as we were driving back to their house, where I would stay until I found my own apartment. I felt a little overwhelmed, but happy to be beginning a new chapter of my life. Soon, I would be in my own apartment and begin my research in Andrew's lab.

While my aunt and everyone else was out at work or school, I had the house to myself. One of the first things I did was sneak into Auntie Cathy and Uncle John's bathroom. There was a scale. I stepped on gingerly. 137. I was disgusted with myself. How could I have ballooned from a low of 106 the summer before to this fat weight? No wonder even my "fat" clothes were too tight to wear.

I stepped off the scale, went into Sarah's room and flopped down on the guest bed. The Voices bombarded me with criticism for the weight gain. "You fat pig. Bitch, you can't even control your weight, and you wish to control Us?" They laughed cruelly. "Die! Die!"

As I lay there, assaulted by the Voices and the self-loathing They inspired, I slipped into the state of mind that taught me the Deep Meaning. Trying to get my thoughts together, I pulled out my computer and began typing. Writing soothed me as it channelled the Messages of the Deep Meaning and the bombardment of Voices:

Perfect points of purest light appear... there is a hidden, mysterious meaning in Them, a meaning that so far eludes me. Each appearance attended to brings me nearer the Deep Meaning, and I crave Their appearance now....

They must know the true truth....

They tell me that I am guilty. Of what, exactly, I'm not sure, as They only say guilty! guilty! guilty! and do not state my crime. Partly, it is letting my grandfather die in front of me, but there is more than that to be guilty of, They say....

My logical mind says no, to suicide is not right. But it only has access to common sense and human knowledge. It cannot begin to penetrate the Deep Meaning, just like other people, so well-meaning when they say I must not even think on suicide. They do not know the Deep Meaning either.

I was again entering into the land of the Voices and learning Their Deep Meaning. I realized that I was chosen, the only one allowed to learn the Deep Meaning. Later, I wrote more:

The main problem now is the rats that are eating my brain. I know that by common sense this cannot be occurring, but by the Deep Meaning I know it is happening....

They have begun on the cerebral cortex, and can only be halted by higher brain processes.... So, this is why I must not to go to sleep, so that I can keep the cerebral cortex neurons firing and thus prevent the rats from consuming them. They get electrocuted from the electricity of firing neurons....

The rats are actually very small, on the same scale as the neurons and they eat them one at a time... I don't know what colour they are, because my vision for my brain is in black and white....

The doctors wouldn't have realized that I have rats in my brain from the tests they did, since the rats are too small to be seen on a CT scan, and do not interfere with the electrical activity as picked up by EEG; their work is too slow, one neuron at a time. And doctors only have access to normal knowledge; they cannot know the Deep Meaning, so only I know that rats are eating my brain.

Unfortunately, small goats sometimes graze on my optic nerves. They eat quite sizable pieces, but the nerves can regenerate, luckily.... The goats first came when I was in the hospital, and one of the nurses said "goats" and then I knew that it was a sign letting me realize that they were beginning....

They tell me that I must take a medication for "the treatment of psychosis and the symptoms of schizophrenia." But they simply do not know the Deep Meaning, and think it is an illness needing treatment.

I reread this lengthy jumble of thoughts. Hallucinations and delusions reigned as I wrote and as I read it now, I see that some makes no sense. It is disconnected, often following tangents that only schizophrenic me could make sense of. Rats? Goats? Deep Meaning? These made perfect sense to me before, but now, distanced by anti-psychotic drugs, I am confused by what I wrote. And yet, at the time, it had all made perfect sense to me. I didn't question it then. I accepted what the Voices and Deep Meaning said because that was my reality.

* * *

That June of 2002, I arrived at Dr. Schwartz's Vancouver office tagged with a diagnosis of paranoid schizophrenia from the NS. My outpatient psychiatrist at the NS back East had referred me to him and had set up an initial appointment at UBC Hospital. I remember little other than sitting silently on a small couch in his office as he probed with questions until announcing that he was going to certify me. Now. I had unwittingly told of my suicide ideation and plans: when the Voices said the time was right, I was to take a rope and ladder from Auntie Cathy's garage and again try to hang myself. I may have also talked about schizophrenic things, such as rats and the Deep Meaning, which also would have led to an immediate hospitalization.

My disease had managed to follow me all the way across the country.

I was put into a seclusion room. Anguished, I felt the rats and heard the Voices. "Brain eaters! Now you pay for your sins!" They screamed. I fled to the concrete wall and began banging my head on it. As my forehead became swollen and sore, bleeding, nurses rushed in. "Stop it, Erin!" they shouted, but I was far away. Soon their medicated needles were poking me and sedation washed over me, through me. Chemical restraints made me so sedated that they didn't immediately put me in the physical bonds. Those would come later, usually after I had bashed my head against a concrete wall. (I had discovered that I could rid myself of rats by bleeding. Denied sharps with which to cut, I became a head-banger.)

Later, I paced my small locked cell, or lay curled up in the fetal position, rocking and sucking my thumb or holding my hands over my ears in a futile attempt to tune the Voices down. Meals came and went; I had lost my appetite. I just wanted *home*. The most comfort I could derive in that tiny cell was to pull my thin mattress over to the corner and press myself into the cold, white walls. There, I slept, until the Voices woke me. They were laughing.

* * *

I had been certified under the Mental Health Act. A copy was pinned to the wall outside my door and one day I read it:

> "In the psychiatrist's opinion, this person: has a disorder of the mind that requires treatment and which seriously impairs the person's ability to react appropriately to his/her environment or to associate with others….[and] requires treatment in or through a designated facility and requires care, supervision and control in or through a designated facility to prevent his/her substantial mental or physical deterioration or for the protection of this person or for the protection of others, and cannot suitably be admitted as a voluntary patient."

I was seriously impaired – by a disorder of the mind? I had deterioration that needed a designated facility? I needed to be controlled? I felt awful, and turned away, wishing I had never read what I just had.

Years later, I would read my charts and find out that I was "in need of medication and talking therapy." I certainly got plenty of the former in hospital, but talking therapy was little more than the psychiatrist's brief list of standard questions: Was I at risk of hurting myself or others? Was I hearing Voices? And, my favourite: Was I delusional? I mean, if I were, it's not as if I could tell, right?

There were also the long, tedious questionnaires. "Have you ever felt you ought to cut down on your use of alcohol, medications, or drugs?" *Yes.* "Have you ever felt guilty about your use of alcohol, medications, or drugs?" *Yes.* However, I now doubt they meant the anti-psychotics I was on, the anti-psychotics that were really making little difference in my symptoms. The Voices shouted at me constantly, sometimes a dozen strong. "She'll die," They would say. "But this is not the time." Soon, though: "She hangs, she hangs, she hangs!" Then, maliciously, They would laugh again.

I began hoarding means of suicide. I found a plastic bag, a possible means to the End. I hid a fork from my tray, and a pin, but the nurse found them. One night, all night, I was put in physical restraints because I could not keep from banging my head on the concrete wall, trying to bleed the rats out. Ironically, they were tying me up *for my safety;* but wouldn't the death of rats be safer than restraints and injections? I struggled against Security and nurses, all four limbs strong. My long hair unkempt, I was wild. I was caught up in a world where rats flooded my brain and where Voices talked of my impending death. So, a few days later, I was sent to the province's psychiatric hospital, Riverview, as a high suicide and elopement risk, and needing "complex case management."

72

*   *   *

I had been admitted to UBC hospital June 25th and transferred to Riverview ICU – British Columbia's version of Nova Scotia's NS - July 2nd. The psychiatrist at Riverview, Dr. Ketch, evaluated my medications and decided to switch me over from olanzapine to clozapine. I was eager to try this new drug, given that I had gained almost 25 pounds in half a year on the olanzapine (a common side effect of anti-psychotics in general, and olanzapine in particular). I was now a fat girl of 144 pounds. While I was concentrating on this factor, the doctor told me that he was putting me on clozapine for refractory psychosis. In other words, I was not responding to medication; two other medications had not kept my schizophrenia in check. Most often, clozapine will help when other drugs have failed. Due to some potentially lethal side-effects of clozapine that involve the immune system, to start the drug there were two official requirements:

1. Non-responsive to treatment with appropriate courses of two chemically unrelated anti-psychotic drugs used for an adequate duration (usually a 6-week trial for each).
2. Intolerance: the inability to achieve adequate benefit with conventional anti-psychotic drugs.

That was me.

Would this new drug help me escape from a lifetime of schizophrenia's psychosis? A part of me held on to it, unsure what I would do without it. The Voices were quite compelling and the Deep Meaning powerful; I felt I must comply with them. I listened to the psychiatrist's theory that they were "internally generated by my own mind," but knew he didn't have an inkling of the magnitude of the

Deep Meaning and all its accompaniments.

Dr. Ketch questioned me of other things: my happiness (three out of ten), and the auditory hallucination of Voices Who had shown me the place to hang myself in my aunt's garage. "The Voices say I'll die," I told him quietly but with fear. As he continued interrogating me about my symptoms, I withdrew. I was distressed and defensive, hiding my face and clinging to my chair. I just wanted to be left alone. "Bad specimen she is!" "Stupid she is!" They kept repeating, distracting me from what Dr. Ketch was saying, and laughing evilly at me throughout. At last, he stopped his analyzing and let me go.

He asked me if it would be alright to contact my parents. I shrugged. Later, he reported back the conversation to me: in sum, they were very quiet and not at all forthcoming. In fact, they were silent, waiting for him to say something. Dr. Ketch found this very odd and cold. But why should they start the conversation? Dr. Ketch was the one with the agenda, not them. So while he used the brief call as evidence of a disturbed childhood for me, I thought that my parents were simply introverted and willing to listen. Psychiatry, it seems, loves to read parental neglect in any silence. Dr. Ketch called it his "theory of inadequate parenting." The nerve.

*   *   *

Despite my issues with Dr. Ketch, I decided to reveal some of my paintings to him, which apparently indicated "clear evidence that [I] had been subjected to boundary violation and, by definition, sexual abuse as a teenager." Furthermore, they suggested that I had experienced "betrayal trauma" as an "extremely vulnerable individual." Although I would later disagree with some of Dr. Ketch's ideas, these hit close. As a teenager, one of my high-school teachers, Chris, abused me sexually and emotionally. There is no shred of doubt in my mind that Chris had violated my boundaries. My trusting and naïve nature did leave me immensely vulnerable, especially since I had been suicidal and paranoid when she first met me. These many years later, I have become convinced that what she did to me was criminal and that she deserves to be prosecuted legally; in 2009, I phoned the police and an investigation was begun.

I had few visitors at Riverview and those that did come, no matter good intentions or family ties, stressed me into further illness. I couldn't handle it. After a visitor left, I immediately dissociated and ran, cowering, to a corner. There was always such safety in a corner. Then I would become unresponsive to staff for an hour or more. If my favourite nurse, Aimee, was on shift, she would sit with me and talk soothingly until I came through. Other staff either left me alone or tried to goad me out of it, making it worse.

"She is unable to act or respond. Her defences are overwhelmed," Aimee wrote after drawing me back to the world. For good measure, though, they always escorted me back into one of the Quiet Rooms.

"Here, Erin," Aimee said quietly, handing me a steaming cup of tea in a Styrofoam cup on one such day. I had been huddled on the floor of the Quiet Room, until this small act of kindness was offered to me. How many hours had I spent there? The staff at Riverview was generally harsh and cold, but Aimee seemed like she actually cared. She took me for walks on Riverview's beautiful, expansive lawns, and we talked. She shared things from her own personal life, a rarity for psych ward staff, and asked me questions about my "real" life – not just the parts that had been claimed by my schizophrenia. She was young, not much older than I was, and happy in her life. It was hard to have her leave at the end of her shifts, let alone when I would leave Riverview to go back to UBC. Her kindnesses have not been forgotten.

*　　*　　*

My most vivid memory of Riverview is that of boredom. We were allowed but minimal time in our rooms, and the TV in the common area was not on until after 4:00 in the afternoon. The only activity was colouring. I tired of that quickly. Mostly, I slept awkwardly on the common room chairs, along with many of the other patients. We would pull over a footstool, align it with a chair, and stretch half-way out. It wasn't very comfortable, but being so heavily medicated meant that I could sleep almost anywhere: I was "sloth-like." The clozapine made me drool, and I was embarrassed – despite being ignored by patients and staff alike – to find a little puddle under my cheek each time I woke up.

I interacted little with the other patients. I preferred my own little world of Deep Meaning. Moreover I obsessed over what I was – and wasn't – eating. I timed my daily shower with the end of afternoon snack, which was usually something high-calorie and low-nutrient such as donuts or cookies. In the shower, I purged down the drain, pushing the mush I vomited through the little holes. That is but one example of how desperate a bulimic can be: you touch your own vomit. But that was the best way I could think of to get rid of the food, so I did it.

Throughout the stay, the main issue and the reason for the transfer in the first place, was my suicidality. I constantly scanned the environment for ways to kill myself and unwittingly shared this with staff. This led to either "territorial confinement" (Quiet Room), restraints (physical and chemical), or "constant attention" (nurse one-to-one).

Not fun. It got to the point where I would simply deny suicide ideation, no matter whether it was the truth or not; I hated the punishments. Besides, it was the Voices and the Deep Meaning that wanted me to kill myself, not *me*.

Finally, the staff at Riverview deemed me stable enough to return to UBC's psych ward. Still, my "overall insight" was "questionable," as was my "judgement." Before I left, Dr. Ketch handed me a copy of his transfer-out summary, which I read with interest. Apparently, I had been grinning inappropriately, yet denied the presence of emotions. The writing I had shared was declared bizarre and pseudophilosophical with persecutory beliefs and ideas of reference. It was little surprise, then, that I was declared impaired to the degree of being unable to function adequately in social and vocational aspects of my life.

I certainly did not agree with Dr. Ketch that my childhood was a "cold, lonely, barren, and unemotional place to be." Yet this was his opinion and from this, he diagnosed reactive attachment disorder of early childhood (RAD). He thought that I satisfied Criterion I of the diagnosis, a "persistent failure to initiate or respond in a developmentally-appropriate fashion to social interactions." Although I admitted that, despite my attempts, I had poor social skills, I didn't think it warranted such a diagnosis. Additionally, I, in Dr. Ketch's opinion, met two or three criteria from borderline personality disorder, one from avoidant personality disorder, a couple from dissociative personality disorder, and one from dependent personality disorder... but doesn't everyone? As for the RAD, who didn't have imperfect parents? And who didn't, in adolescence, balk at attachment gestures such as hugs from parents? I am insulted that he drew such erroneous and accusative conclusions about me and my family. Moreover, if he did not think I had schizophrenia, then why did he put me on clozapine, a drug used almost exclusively for the treatment of schizophrenia?

*   *   *

At UBC, after the inter-hospital transfer, they plied me with questions for an assessment. Again. How do you know when you are ill? *Don't know.* What are you concerned about now? *Leaving hospital.* What are your expectations of this hospitalization? *I don't know.* Occasionally I refused to answer ("poverty of thought," they recorded); later I would read that not only was my affect "blunt," but it was "blunt +++." At times, I required physical touch to be alerted to the conversation. I cared only to spend most of my time in the fetal position on my bed, which I had moved to a corner. I was still very much in the bonds of my schizophrenia.

"The time has come," the Voices informed me. "Time to die." The Voices kept telling me to cut, and though I feared scars, I obeyed with anything sharp I could find, such as a thumbtack off the information board. I refused medication, was wary of the orange juice they offered; "I don't know what's in it," I told the nurses. I was frightened, eyes wide and fingers twisting the hem of my pyjama shirt.

"Come now, Erin," the nurse said again, but gently. "You need these medications. Please take them."

"But if I take too many meds, or the wrong ones, the rats will come to eat my brain again," I replied, terrified. I could not take my eyes off the medication in the little cup she held out to me.

"Erin, you must take these pills. I can assure you, there are no rats in them."

I did not believe her. "How can you know that for sure when you don't even know the Deep Meaning?" I lashed out.

She was losing her patience with me. "Erin, if you don't take these pills, I will have to give them to you with a needle. You don't want that, do you." It was not a question.

"I can't," I wailed. "No."

"Syringe, then." She walked away, reappearing moments later with the dreaded needle. Well, if that was what she was going to do, then I would resist in every way I could.

"Code White, 2 North, Code White, 2 North," I heard calmly over the PA system. That was me: aggression. Security came running.

It took four strong Security officers to pin my limbs down while the nurse swabbed, then stabbed, my thigh. "No!" I screamed, struggling in vain to get away. But it had already been done: the medication, riddled with rats, coursed through my body. There was nothing more to do but lie there and sob as they restrained me, left me. I had never felt so alone. I couldn't even wipe my falling tears away.

In the morning, they let me out of the restraints. It was time for another history with yet another psychiatrist, accompanied by the usual resident or student. I showed little emotion, and "contradictory body language" (whatever that was). I admitted to them that I was struggling to keep others from reading my mind, although I didn't think that this was unusual, just terribly frightening and disconcerting. What I didn't realize, though, was that this, too, was a part of my schizophrenia.

I liked my new psychiatrist, Dr. Hij, and even granted him permission to phone my parents. They said that as a child, I was extremely shy and timid, but they acknowledged that I was quite successful in hiding my psychosis, including the Voices I heard so distressingly, from them throughout high school. They were disturbed to hear that I was a head-banger. My mother did note that I shut down during phone calls when I was in, or just about to be admitted to, the hospital.

My lack of expression was diverted, written in bloodied lines on my arms. I had become a cutter, the blood-letting comforting me, but also, more importantly, it bled out the rats. This self-harm would continue to happen whenever I was in a schizophrenic episode; I began to consider the scars to be a sort of corporal diary of what I had been through.

I would have to live with the scars, I knew, but I was just beginning to learn that I also had to come to terms with my diagnosis, to learn to live with the schizophrenia that scarred my brain. Not surprisingly, I was recommended for both group and individual therapy, told that I would require long-term psychotherapy in addition to being medicated for the rest of my life. I was scared. Scared of the psychiatric care – both in and out of hospital – that would make me "better." Scared because the Voices hated it when I was beginning to get better and would shriek at me in fury. "Liar, liar, liar!" They shouted at me. What was I lying about?

*   *   *

By the end of my month-long stay at UBC, the Voices were gone and everything seemed so much easier. I could talk, buy, ask for help again. Records written by Dr. Robbyn, my latest out-patient psychiatrist, quote me as saying that I was feeling the best I ever had.

It wouldn't last.

By October, the Voices were back telling me that "the girl dies... the girl will die." I had gathered together some

80

materials at home in response to my suicide ideation, but told Dr. Robbyn that I wasn't allowed to tell her, unsure of whether or not I could phone her if things got worse. I had regressed to a state of numbness: "minimal to no eye contact, little to no spontaneous outflow of speech, long latency to respond, speech that was hypophonic, generally only responding with single words." She would later describe me as "partially mute." I was "difficult to access."

Nevertheless, I was being very closely monitored by Dr Robbyn, who admitted to being willing (and, of course, able) to re-hospitalize me at any time. I was also being monitored physically, as the clozapine I was taking could lower white blood cell counts – fatally. I was consistently in the "yellow" region of caution, so I had to go twice weekly for blood tests. At end of December of 2002, I was "at serious risk of relapse if medication were to be suddenly discontinued." "Serious" was underlined twice. A month later, I would prove them right.

Chapter 7: Sharps and Scars

The rats had been steadily increasing in number and were taking over my brain. They ate neurons voraciously, greedy and without care for the damage they were inflicting. It was the will of the Deep Meaning, but I tried my every trick to keep the destruction at bay. I studied and worked hard and limited my hours of sleep so that I would be keeping my brain electrified and thus electrocuting as many rats as possible.

Despite this effort, I was enjoying my work at the lab, both academically and socially. I was learning everything from behavioural testing to tissue collection to post-mortem analysis. My favourite was assessing the strength and cognition of the "ALS-PDC" mice. To test their strength, I suspended them from a string; they could hang for quite a while, but to my consternation the smarter ones learned how to swing their hind legs up to the string and hold on by all four limbs, thereby thwarting my assessment of forelimb strength. That was frustrating. Also frustrating were the mice that refused to swim in the water-maze task, where they were supposed to learn that swimming (in warm water) down a certain one of four radial arms led to a platform onto which they could escape the wetness they didn't like. I called these non-swimmers "floaters." Usually, though, things went smoothly.

I also learned what scientists call "bench work." I learned how to prepare tissue samples, ending up with stained slides that I then used to count cells in the spinal cord. Interestingly, I found that cells were not dying, even when the mice were impaired on their tests, suggesting "sick" cells were causing the deficits... which meant that there was the possibility that intervention could be begun before neurons were lost, hopefully allowing those cells to recover.

Socially, I was enjoying being part of the lab. Everyone was friendly, without gossip or judgements. Melissa worked there, and became a close friend with whom I'm still in contact now, years later. As a lab, we'd go out to celebratory lunches for birthdays, and chatted in the lab on slow days. I was accepted for who I was and that made me happy.

Still, the rats in my head gnawed – I could hear it clearly – and the pressure in my skull grew and grew. Finally, I could stand it no longer. If I didn't act now, the damage would be irreparable and the rats victorious. I was in the lab, writing, and simply could not concentrate for all the rats crowding my head. I grabbed a new razor blade from the lab bench and headed to the bathroom. Locked in a stall, I sliced through the thin skin of my left wrist with one quick motion, expecting the usual superficial cut, the minimal blood flow for the removal of the rats. But blood! Pulsing and spurting, the red liquid spattered the walls and floor. The open artery churned out fresh blood by the second and I panicked. Rats drained quickly from the wound, easing the pressure in my head, but I was bleeding heavily enough that I feared passing out and being discovered too late.

I hid there in the stall and pressed endless paper towels to my wrist. Eventually, the flow seemed to have been stemmed. I wiped the pools of blood off the wall and floor and headed directly over to Emergency at Vancouver General Hospital (VGH), only two buildings down the street from the lab. As I suspected, the depth of the cut required stitches, but, despite my telling of rats and pressure and Deep Meaning and, of course, the cutting itself, I was not admitted to the psych ward, or even seen by a psychiatrist. I walked back to the lab, collected my things, and headed home.

Although I was becoming more and more delusional, I had the presence of mind to recognize a need for some sort of psychiatric intervention. I assumed that if I went to see Dr. Robbyn she would increase my clozapine and let me go home. I was wrong.

"Erin, I think you need to be in the hospital," she said softly. She saw that I was experiencing considerable distress, with, as she noted, a "decreasing ability to control or resist impulses." I told her that the Voices of the Deep Meaning were planning to have me killed, because it was the Right Thing.

I was frightened. Part of me agreed with her that I needed to go into the hospital – I had seen what my beliefs had led to this time – but another part of me thought otherwise. That part spoke.

"No, not the hospital," I pleaded, but she was adamant. She picked up the phone on her desk.

"Hello? Yes, this is Dr. Robbyn from Psychiatry. I have a patient here that I think needs to be hospitalized."

She listened a moment. "Okay, I'll bring her over." I knew it was decided. Dr. Robbyn led me out of the clinic and to Emergency and I followed meekly.

She sat me down in the waiting area and went to talk to the admitting nurse. There were only two people there ahead of me, so it would be a short wait. Dr. Robbyn sat down beside me, but checked her watch every few minutes. Finally, she stood up. "I have to go for my next patient," she announced. After a brief comment with the nurse at the desk, it was decided that she would watch me. Dr. Robbyn left.

Unsure of what would happen to me, I sat, scared, in my waiting-room seat. The nurse glanced up at me often, but there was really no need to keep watch. Where would I go? They'd certainly find me and it might make everything worse than it already was, so I sat.

"Erin? They're ready for you," the nurse called. I rose, went in. It was crowded in Emergency, and instead of being brought to a bed, I was led to a closet-sized seclusion room. My bed was a thin foam mattress that took up most of the space on the concrete floor. A nurse gave me some hospital pyjamas and left me to change; another nurse took my vitals. A doctor came in and crouched near my mattress.

"Hi, Erin," he said. "Can you tell me a bit about why you're here?"

"I tried to get the rats out," I began. "There were so many, and I couldn't think."

"Why not?"

"They were eating my brain faster than it could regenerate," I answered.

"Oh?"

"Yeah, there were so many of them," I repeated. "I

had to get them out."

"How?"

"That's why I cut my wrist open. They come out in the blood."

"So that wasn't an attempt to kill yourself, or even a suicidal gesture?"

"No, it wasn't. I was just dealing with the rats."

"Hmm." I waited for his next question. "I see from your records that you've been in hospital before, Erin. UBC and Riverview."

"Yes. Last year."

"What for? Do you know your diagnosis?" I wasn't sure what to answer. I had received such different opinions from different doctors. Schizophrenia was the most common one, but Dr. Ketch's diagnoses were also in my chart.

"I'm not sure," I replied.

"Dr. Robbyn certified you, and she wrote down a diagnosis of schizophrenia," he offered. I nodded sadly. "And given what you've told me I'd be inclined to agree with her," he added. "I think it's a good idea for you to be in hospital a little while, Erin." We talked a few minutes more and then he left, charting that I was in the midst of a "situational crisis." My insight was "partial to impaired" and my judgement "compromised." When well, I would agree, but in the moment, I thought I was appropriate. That is, appropriate in the context of my hallucinations and delusions.

That little seclusion room with its uncomfortable mattress was my room for the entire weekend. I took my meals there, the only points of interest of the day. I had phoned to tell Melissa and Daniel, my friends from the lab, that I'd been hospitalized. Daniel came by to visit. He surveyed my "room," somewhat appalled. It couldn't be helped, though. There were no beds available on the psych ward that Friday, and discharges do not take place on the weekend. Monday a bed became available on Ward 2 North.

"We'll be changing your medication, Erin," I was told by one of the ward psychiatrists after I was transferred. "We're going to try a newer drug, quetiapine, otherwise known as Seroquel, instead of the clozapine. Your blood work shows that the clozapine has lowered your white blood cell counts to dangerously low levels, which puts you at risk of agranulocytosis. That is a potentially fatal condition in which the immune system cannot fight off infections." He paused. "The Seroquel should have fewer side effects and more efficacy than the clozapine you're on now. We'll start you on it tonight at 50 mg, and increase it every day or two until you reach a therapeutic dose. Usually, it's between 300 mg and 800 mg a day."

I took the information in. This would be the fourth anti-psychotic I'd tried. I hoped that this one would work, and for longer than the seven months I'd been on the clozapine. At least this one wouldn't require weekly blood tests.

On the ward, nothingness filled my days while the Voices screamed at me. I would rock myself, cover my ears, hum in a monotone – anything to try and get them to quiet down. "Are you hearing things?" the staff would query and all I could do was nod. The Voices yelled Their Plans for me to die – "She is bad. She is done for." – but I didn't want to die, even if it was the Right Thing. Still, it was so hard to resist. "Ambivalent intent," the nurses wrote.

Moreover, the rats remained. Not all had drained through that slit in my wrist. I tried to ignore them, but they persisted and even multiplied. I had nothing with which to cut; I had to start head banging again. It would break through the thin skin on my forehead, leaking rats out. I positioned myself in front of the concrete wall, pulled my head backwards, and jerked it forward with force. Thwack! It crashed into the unyielding wall. Thud, thud, thud. More contact. With every bash, I calmed. Rhythmic. Dull pain. A thin line of rat-filled blood trickled down the baby-blue concrete.

"Erin! Stop that!" Nurses came quickly, alerted by the noise. "Erin, you have to stop. You're hurting yourself." They pulled me forcibly away.

"Let me go!" I pleaded. "The rats. I have to get them out!" I struggled against their grasp.

"No, Erin. Look, if you can't stop on your own, we'll have to restrain you. You don't want that, do you?"

"Noooo," I cried. "No, please, just let me go." And I flung myself out of their hands and into the bloodstained wall. A resounding *thud* echoed in the small room.

Security was on their way, and, once in their hold, I was unable to move. The restraint bed, adorned on its four corners with shackles, was brought in and I was flung onto it. Crying, I pleaded with them. "Please don't tie me up, please!"

"You gave us no choice," was the harsh answer. Also of no choice: injections.

"No!" I screamed. "No! No! Not the rats! Please, please, don't inject me with the rats! No!"

"Don't be silly, we're not injecting rats into you," someone said condescendingly. Then another, younger voice piped up.

"Oh, can I watch? I've never seen one of these before," squeaked a medical student who had wandered into the room. Oh look, this guinea pig is a novel show. Fuck you, I thought, but then pleaded with her to help me.

"They're injecting rats into me," I cried at her.

I was quickly, expertly secured. "Can you hold her leg over so I can give her an injection?" a nurse asked. Strong male hands thrust me over, exposing my buttocks. A prick, and the Ativan flowed into my system. No, not again. I sensed the rats: hundreds and thousands of tiny rats flowed in the Ativan into my system. They could do that to me? Inject me with rats as a punishment for trying to get rid of the few rats that remained in me? I felt betrayed. I felt aghast. I felt defeated. I cried, softly and hopelessly. The rat-infested Ativan soon gave its strong sedation and then I slept.

* * *

Days began to blur. My forehead scabbed over. I was quiet and kept to myself, pacing the circular ward endlessly. I read, I played chess with myself (or just put the pieces on and took them off again, over and over again). I cared little about my appearance and was dishevelled and unkempt. I ate my three meals a day.

My bulimia had followed me into the hospital. Carefully and quietly, I retreated to my bathroom a couple times a day to vomit. I weighed myself every morning on the scale. It was thankfully hidden in the laundry room, so the nurses didn't know. My little secret.

I was very wary of staff and their endless questions. I was charted as "mute, sluggish/slow, shows little/no feelings." With the other patients and my (few) visitors I was a bit more animated, but only because I feared them less than I feared the staff. Daily, the Voices yelled, angry, at me for not harming myself, but I felt safe because I knew They did not want me to do anything in public. Still, my psychiatrist thought that it was only a matter of time before I hurt myself again.

They were right. Somehow, I acquired two needles: one, a sewing needle, and one, the kind with which they filled me with Ativan and rats. "The time is coming to do this," the Voices told me. I soon had several small cuts on my right wrist.

I didn't want to be one of those girls who self-harmed for attention. I cut because I feared rats, wanted to bleed them out. I was scaring myself, though; on a pass, I bought a sharp Exacto knife. The Voices were happy – "Cut now, please!" – but I feared another incident like the one a few weeks earlier.

So I showed the nurse my knife, willingly giving it up. "The Voices made me do it," I pleaded, fearing punishment in the form of rat-infested Ativan. She saw the 20 or so small cuts on my right wrist, but simply talked to me.

"It is a good thing, you bringing in your sharps to me," she said calmly. "However, I need you to contract to me for your safety: that you will not bring any more in, whether you buy them on pass or bring them from home, and you will turn in any others you might have in your room now."

"I can try," I said honestly.

"I need better than try. I need you to contract, verbally, now."

I sighed. The Voices weren't liking this. They liked to see me bleed, hoping it would culminate in suicide, the ultimate fate They had for me.

"Okay," I whispered. Voices were yelling already but I could be stronger than Them. I had to be. "I contract."

"Good. Now let me have a look at your wrist and

clean it," she said. She took my hand gently in her own. Little rivulets of red blood criss-crossed my wrist but there was no pain. She cleaned it, bandaged it, and left me in my room.

After every pass from then on I had to answer the sharps question. At some point I had the sutures removed from my left wrist. While the wounds on my right wrist would prove too superficial to leave a permanent mark, I was left with a white scar on my left. I now look at it from time to time, a memory of the rats and everything else it represents. It is a warning: *take your meds.*

*   *   *

Psychology decided to assess me. He came with his papers, endless questionnaires. I sat, in "childlike posture," looking much younger than my 23 years, and listened. My lack of communication made it impossible to assess my mood, associations, fluency, thought content, and other abnormalities often present in schizophrenia.

Rorschach testing – the infamous "ink blots" - drew out bizarre and morbid responses, at least in the opinion of the psychologist. I simply said what I saw. I suppose now that living in a delusional ("bizarre") state and being constantly told by the Voices that I should be suicidal ("morbid") made their mark. The assessment concluded that, in contrast to Dr. Ketch's assumptions, I indeed suffered from schizophrenia. My psychosis was deemed "genuine." I was, in his words, "a very fragmented individual."

I wasn't sure what to make of the comment that I was fragmented, but the word genuine meant a lot to me. Sometimes, when I am well, it all just seems like it is a farce, a play, a fake. When well, I read back over these pages I've written – which are as honest and accurate as possible – or through the hospital notes, and it is as if it were a dream (nightmare?). Did I really believe I had rats in my brain? Was I really cutting to let those rats out, or was it a more usual explanation: attention? Maybe I just made it all up.

But then I remember. Remember my panic at the Ativan injections. Remember my distress when the Voices would yell. Remember just how hard it was to go day to day. Then reality sets in. I am sick. Anti-psychotics make things like rats and Voices virtually disappear, even though I never believed that this would happen. Ergo: schizophrenia. Right?

I was faithfully taking my Seroquel but it was not enough. I was paranoid. Like so many schizophrenics I believed that I was under surveillance. "The Watcher" kept tabs on me, I realized one day a few weeks after being discharged from the hospital. It was unnerving but not menacing. I was told by the Deep Meaning that he lived in an apartment across the alley from me and could see into my apartment through the sheer curtains on my windows. He was more curious than threatening but it still frightened me. After another week or so, though, I learned (again, by the Deep Meaning, of course) that he intended to kill me. Soon. In my delusional and paranoid state, I was terrified.

Chapter 8: The Homicidal Tracker

Over the weeks following my return home from the hospital, I became more and more aware of the Watcher. Then, the day after I took down my sheer curtains and put up dark brown ones, the Watcher became the Tracker. Unlike the white curtains I had taken down, these new drapes were opaque, effectively hiding my position from the Watcher. I felt a safety, an obscurity, with the brown barrier hanging between me and the Watcher. I was quite certain that he could not see me; why I thought this would thwart his intent to murder me – that he would simply give up and let me live in peace – I don't know.

It was during the next night, in May of 2003, that the Watcher put his bugs in my apartment and his tracker in my stomach. Now, there was absolutely no hiding; I was under 24-hour surveillance. The frustrating part was that the bugs were invisible, which meant that any recourse to the police would be fruitless. I only knew that they were there because the Deep Meaning had revealed it to me. The Deep Meaning also explained to me how the Watcher had gotten them into my locked apartment. Apparently, he possessed an atomizer gun, a device that (as the Deep

Meaning told me) broke any item into its component atoms, passed them through a barrier (in this case, the glass of my patio door) and then caused the atoms to reassemble into their original order on the other side.

Worse than the bugs was the tracker. The Watcher-turned-Tracker had atomized a small tracking device into my stomach while I slept that Saturday night. It emitted a signal that the Tracker could use to locate me even behind the obscurity of the brown curtains. More than that, he could now track me wherever I went. Sunday, I was dimly aware that something had happened, but it wasn't until the next morning that I really clued into what had transpired.

I awoke Monday morning knowing that I could not go into work, that there was something in connection with the Deep Meaning that required urgent attention. I packed my bag for work, intending to go there in the afternoon, after I had figured out what was going on, and then left to wander the streets to look for clues. In the past, I had been given insight into the Deep Meaning by the "Signs and Evidence" coded in little things I found on the street; every little thing had intense and specific Meaning. That day, I found an unbroken red elastic band, meaning that next time I would try to commit suicide it wouldn't involve cutting my wrist or otherwise bleeding out. This was a relief, but I knew that it wasn't what the Deep Meaning was trying to communicate to me that morning.

As I sat in a café sipping hot coffee, I began to realize what was going on. The Deep Meaning revealed to me that the Watcher was tracking me, and that I needed to find a safe place to stay for a couple of days, until I sorted out how to outsmart him. If I didn't, it would only be a matter of time before he shot me, or I killed him out of fear and self-defense. It would be difficult, given that I would not recognize him on the street. (I had never actually seen him. I didn't need to, for the Deep Meaning told me everything I was required to know.)

My first refuge was a narrow staircase leading up from a lobby to second-story offices on Elm Street. I napped a Seroquel nap (easily done given Seroquel's significant sedation) there for a while, ignored by the few people passing up or down the staircase. I was hearing strange sounds, though; sounds like machines grinding through the building's concrete assaulted my ears every so often, eventually convincing me that I was not safe there.

I left, following my intuition eastward along the alleyway. The Tracker could pick up my signal easily, and I knew I was in danger. As I approached (VGH), I decided to go in to get another coffee there and try to think things through, knowing that the thick concrete walls would, as they did in the staircase on Elm Street, afford me some protection from the Tracker. I sat, thinking. The walls blocked the signal from my tracking device, but I knew that it would only be a matter of time before he realized that, too. He would then program the tracker to emit stronger signals.

As I focused on the signal being sent out from my abdomen, I suddenly realized how many electronic machines were in use at the hospital, each emitting signals of their own. My ears were flooded with whirling, beeping, static-y signals, confirming my hunch. It was here, in the hospital, that I could hide from the Tracker! Between the concrete walls that blocked, and the cacophony of mechanical noises that confused, my signal was effectively scrambled beyond recognition. I was safe!

So then the task was finding a place within this

hospital haven where I could live, at least for a couple of days until I found a more long-term solution. I remembered the staircase I often took up to the hospital cafeteria. It was large, and I had only ever encountered one or two people on the stairs; I could sleep there. I could use the hospital bathrooms, and eat at the hospital's coffee shop or cafeteria. Perfect, I thought, as I curled up on the dusty concrete floor of the stairwell's landing. Once again, I had been able to discern the Deep Meaning of my situation and would be rewarded accordingly. Strangely, the Voices were unusually quiet.

That staircase, however, was used more often than I had thought. The people passed by without comment, which I interpreted as meaning that they somehow dimly realized that I had outwitted the Tracker and that my intent to live there in that dark corner was incredibly in tune with the Deep Meaning. I was surprised, then, to be awoken by a Security guard not more than two hours later. She gruffly told me that I had to leave. I was confused – didn't she realize that I had to stay there? I tried to convey that message via thought-waves, but she didn't seem at all receptive. "Come on," she said. "You have to leave."

I followed her meekly, figuring that she would just lead me to another place in the hospital in which I could stay. As she guided me down the corridor towards the west-facing doors, though, I halted. Just a block straight out those doors was the Tracker's apartment, and I knew that he would pick up my signal as soon as I went out.

"I have to stay here," I said anxiously.

"You can't stay in a hospital unless you are under a doctor's care," she replied. "Do you want to see a doctor?"

"No." Couldn't she see my predicament? But then, I remembered, she probably had no idea of the Deep

Meaning. Instead, she called for backup, and soon two more Security guards where there. Unsure of whether I needed to be expelled from the building or brought in for treatment, they pelted me with questions. Was I a street kid on drugs? (I guess my sleeping in the dirty stairwell coupled with my attire of old jeans and sweatshirt with its hood pulled low over my eyes gave them that impression.) Did I want to see a doctor? How old was I? What was my name?

I answered only one of their questions. "Julie," I murmured in response to the last query. I couldn't remember if that was my name, or if the Deep Meaning and the Voices had just planted it into my brain. Maybe the Security guards thought my name was Julie, and I needed to acknowledge this fact. The rest of their questions were weighing me down. Security began to physically force me towards the door.

Panic flooded into me. They were going to give me up to the Tracker, who would then kill me before I figured out another safe place to hide – or I might have to kill him! I fought against them, desperate. I guess they began to think that I probably needed help, and let me resist. I stood there rigidly, eyes tightly shut and fists clenched in front of my face. They demanded to see my eyes, to see if drug use would be written in the size of my pupils. No, no, no; they were going to look into my eyes and see my mind and tell the Tracker and maybe even set the rats on me. "Resist the Enemy," the Voices chanted, alternating this command with their pleasure at my success. But the Security guards were strong, and, pinning me to the wall, forced my eyelid open.

"Are you on any drugs?" they demanded.

Thinking that if I just told them a bit, they would let

me go back to my safe stairwell, I answered yes.

"What for – mental illness?" I nodded cautiously. "What, then? Depression? Bipolar? Schizophrenia?" Schizophrenia: that harsh word ripped through my body and mind, and I was again immobilized. They soon had a wheelchair there, and before I knew it, they had lifted me into it and were rolling me down to Emergency. Rifling through my confiscated knapsack, they found ID, and I was dimly aware of them talking to the staff at Emergency. Mentally and emotionally, though, I was far away. I huddled on the floor; I had fled to the floor as soon as the wheelchair had stopped, and they just left me there. I could see a screw in the floor, and I realized why they had brought me there: to liberate the person whose soul lay trapped under the screw. I tried in vain to unscrew it with my keys – which, when they were noticed, were promptly confiscated, too. "I need a screwdriver," I pleaded with one of the Security guards left to keep an eye on me. "Please – I have to let them out. Please."

"Do you want to see a doctor?" he answered.

"No...."

"Then you'll have to leave," he reminded me.

"No – no." I was beginning to panic again. "No – he'll just put rats in my brain. No!"

"They'll admit her," one of the Security guards said to the other. Before long I was a pyjama-clad patient on PAU (Psychiatric Assessment Unit) at VGH. "Found curled in fetal position on main stairwell" read the referral form. I was held initially in one of the four cell-like rooms that were not unlike jail cells: concrete bed frame slightly softened by a thin mattress and, in one corner, a stainless-steel toilet and wash basin. There was also a camera watching me from the ceiling and no doorknob on the inside of the heavy locked door. I stayed there a few days, then graduated to the larger PAU ward where there were normal hospital rooms. (Ironically, the photo of me on the back cover of this book was taken in front of the shrubbery that separates PAU from the street.)

Here I paced round and round the circular ward, balancing everything with rhymes. Mug, rug, plug; floor, door; cup, up; table, able; walk, talk, clock; phone, alone; nurse, purse.... Hearing my sing-song voice and balancing my new home quieted me, but not enough. I needed something more, something that could reach the Deep Meaning. So back to my room and its concrete wall and the familiar rhythm of pain, a rhythm I hoped would at least put the rats to sleep, ideally bleed them out.

The restraints and injections would follow, along with a trip back to the cells.

*   *   *

There was a new patient in cell-room PAU: Richard, a 37-year-old man who was, definitely, Greek, in both appearance (that Mediterranean colouring, such a nice contrast to my pale, pale skin and blue eyes) and personality (assertive, emotional, sensual). He seemed friendly and cheerful, curious but not nosey. He didn't appear to care that I needed my blanket/brain protector that I had begun wearing in the hope that no-one would be then able to read my mind. He did, however, congratulate me when I finally shed it a week later. I felt respected, not judged. When allowed out of our cells into a tiny common area we played cards while he shared generously of the candy his mother brought in, and lived the experience of the cells together. We talked – him at length, with colourful stories, me cautiously, shyly – and ate our hospital meals with plastic cutlery.

I could tell that he liked me.

I wondered whether I liked him. Mostly, I was nearly floored that someone would actually have an interest in me. My self-esteem was so low that I ignored his evident shortcomings, such as his aggression when locked in his room, when he would verbally abuse the staff and throw wet toilet paper onto the plastic dome covering the camera. Instead, I focused on the tingle of excitement when he put his feet up on my chair, just barely touching my thigh. His smile was captivating, his honey-brown eyes drawing me in. I learned that he was diagnosed as bipolar, but this didn't bother me. Being at the tail end of a manic episode, he simply seemed happy, out-going, and personable. We exchanged phone numbers.

Meanwhile, I had been seeing psychiatrists since I was first admitted, but it was a different one every day, it seemed, and it wasn't until the second week that I remembered meeting with any one in particular. Most just wanted to know my story – the resident told one of the nurses who told me that he found it fascinating to talk with me – but one, Dr. Goodwin, went beyond.

She challenged me to accept the diagnosis of schizophrenia, and forced me to admit that though I had good psychological knowledge of schizophrenia (I had, after all, written an award-winning term paper on childhood-onset schizophrenia in university) I had effectively built a fortress of denial: if I were smart enough, studied hard enough, kept up the appearance of normality, then I could not be schizophrenic. Schizophrenics, in my mind, were conspicuously ill, unkempt and anti-social, and I had always prided myself on a neat appearance; their delusions were grandiose, always involving some great figure, such as Jesus Christ or the President, or some great group, such as the CIA or FBI, whereas what psychiatrists called my delusions were great truths based on the Deep Meaning. Dr. Goodwin carefully explained that delusions were as varied as people with schizophrenia, and that I needed to develop the insight that the Deep Meaning and the rats were my delusions. Also, she pointed out that when I was ill I became unkempt and withdrawn. I opened my mind a bit to let her reasonings in, but it was not until later I felt I fully appreciated it.

During other interviews, I was given opportunity to describe to them the sacred yet scientific process of atomization. The Watcher had taken advantage of this technology in order to bug the apartment and insert the tracking device into my abdomen and yet it was also the process by which I could thwart his murderous plans. The Deep Meaning, I told them, had chosen me; it was inevitable, then, that I be shown some profound way of escape. I would myself be atomized.

"What do you mean, atomization? Explain this to me," my doctor of the day enquired.

"For anyone else, atomization would entail death," I began. "For me, it will mean a sort of immortality. My component atoms would become able to rearrange as needed. A bullet, for example, would pass through me without harm, as my atoms would move out of the way and then return to their places." Somehow, I didn't apply this logic to the potential of being shot by the Tracker and still feared him.

"And how do you get atomized?"

"A prerequisite to my atomization appear to you – that is, to all people, since only I have access into the Deep Meaning – as suicide. Probably an overdose or a hanging. Remember, the Deep Meaning had revealed by the Signs and Evidence of the Great Experiment that it would not be by opening an artery again."

"When will this happen? Is it necessary?" the psychiatrist asked, increasingly concerned.

"I'll need to contact the Organ Donor people about that," I answered without elaboration. It was sometimes hard to remember that ordinary people did not have access the Deep Meaning, that they would not immediately see the significance and repercussions of that statement. She probed further, and I readily explained. "Once I am atomized, I will no longer need my organs, and would like to donate them. So, I'll call the Organ Donor people, find out which method of death is most conducive to successful organ donation, and then alert them to the fact that my organs will soon be available. They might have some recipient in mind, so I'd atomize when they said it would be most convenient. Oh, but I will keep my skin and eyeballs, so that I will appear un-atomized to the normal person." I felt confident that my explanation made absolute sense.

"But if you are atomized and have no inner organs, how will your body retain its shape?" she said. What I do not remember her saying, but that she recorded in her notes, was that I seemed surprised when she suggested that the people in organ donation wouldn't give out such information.

She had obviously not understood the profound truth I had taken pains to explain, even though she noted that I had a "very broad and elaborate delusional system." She wrote that I would get mildly irritated when my beliefs were challenged and that they remained rigid. Moreover, I was a suicide risk, via "delusional precepts."

"Don't you see? It is of the Deep Meaning, which

transcends normal logic. Everything of the Deep Meaning is intrinsically true." And as had happened before with so many psychiatrists, she went on to call my knowledge of the Deep Meaning delusion and the Voices that confirmed its Truths hallucinations.

"Tell me about the Watcher." Obviously she had not met with me before, or had not been diligent in remembering notes from my chart.

"He lives in the gravel house." Another profound statement, which of course required no elaboration due to its profundity. (It referred to the fact that the Tracker's building was covered in pebble-like concrete.)

"What?"

"The gravel house. Behind my apartment. He watches me and wants to kill me."

"So he is a real person? Have you seen him? How do you know he is watching you, and that he wants to harm you?"

"Well, he put the Famous Yesterdays in place, so I know he is watching me. And yes, he is real – he will shoot me dead with his rifle if I don't atomize myself in time."

"The Famous Yesterdays?" Her utter lack of insight into the Deep Meaning was obvious. Rather than convince me of the Deep Meaning's delusional quality, this ignorance of hers further told me that it was to me, and me alone, that the Deep Meaning was revealed. She was so dense she couldn't even see the obvious connection: the Watcher had put bugs in my apartment; beetles are bugs; the Beatles are a homophonic form of the word beetles; the Beatles are Famous for their song, Yesterday; the "Famous Yesterdays" was obviously the profound way to say that my apartment was bugged.

She decided to increase my Seroquel 200 milligrams

a day, from the recommended highest dose of 800 mg to 1,000 mg.

*   *   *

As had happened with other medication increases, the Voices decreased in frequency, intensity, and relevance over the next few weeks. They would pipe up a couple times a day. "We're looking for Erin, Erin Hawkes," the older, male Voice called. "Where is she? We need to find her." Later, "Let's see her diagnosis." Nevertheless I seemed stable enough, and so they decided to send me over to UBC hospital.

This was my fourth visit to UBC's psych wards, and both nurses and doctors remembered me. I looked much better than last time, they all noted; indeed, I *was* doing well. The Voices still spoke to me now and then – "Do you have Bible study?" "The Snuddlepuffer." – but it was inconsequential. In fact, my psychiatrist was soon ready to release me, provided I had a successful pass home for a couple hours.

Discharge. Going home. This scared me; I didn't feel stable enough to handle the Tracker, the Famous Yesterdays, the rats, and atomization if they returned in earnest. Restless and anxious, I paced the all-too familiar circle of the ward.

Some pamphlets on schizophrenia caught my eye, and I paused to skim their contents. Two statistics leapt out at me. One in ten: one in ten children of a schizophrenic parent will develop the disease. One in ten schizophrenics will successfully commit suicide. One in ten, one in ten. Put them together and it is one in a hundred, a one percent chance of my having a schizophrenic child who successfully kills him- or herself.

It set me off thinking of other implications my

disease had for the dream I had had forever, of having children, a family. One in ten. One in a hundred. Moreover, what would I do about medication while pregnant? Breastfeeding – no, that was out I sadly realized. And how could I expect to raise children when I myself may become psychotic and so lost in my own reality that I am unable to care for them? Like John Nash as portrayed in the movie, *A Beautiful Mind*, would I become so caught up in the world of schizophrenia that I'd leave my baby unattended in a tub quickly filling with bath water?

Maybe, maybe not. I couldn't tell at this point. I knew by now that I would need to marry someone extremely stable. But who would want a wife so vulnerable to hallucination, delusion, and paranoia?

*   *   *

I awoke the next morning early – around five – and restless. I prayed that the restlessness was just nervousness about my pass and possible discharge, and not the beginnings of akathisia, that unbearable side effect that I had experienced most painfully when I had been on risperidone. As I left the ward on my pass, though, it seemed to just be a bit of anxiety.

The pass went well. I went to the lab and my apartment, trying to judge whether I was ready to be thrust back to the "outside." Nothing was glaringly out of place, but something was just not right. I felt as I had felt over a year earlier in Halifax, when I was on a pass that was to be my last one before discharge; stressed, I was again vulnerable to the Voices' suggestions that I hang myself. Vulnerability: that's what I was again feeling. Stable enough now, but vulnerable. Knowing what it had culminated in before, I was afraid. So I decided to stay in hospital.

While the Tracker and his surveillance system had decreased in importance to me, I still believed that this was due to such things as him going away on business or the bugs being turned off. Likewise, the rats weren't gone; they were simply sleeping. The Voices weren't as intrusive, persistent, or negative as they had been, but they still piped up now and then. They were into rhymes: "Flyin' high, Sugarpie." "Screw you, Buttershoe." "Shut up, Buttercup." Or, nonsense: "What shape can I ask you?"

"Hi! Could you think here, please," the older woman Voice said the next day. I *was* thinking, thinking about how I could help convey to other people the experience of schizophrenia. Particularly, I had my parents and sister in mind. For most of my illness, I had shared virtually nothing with my parents other than the emotionless stats of my changing medication types and dosages and the earning of passes. I knew this hurt them, but until I had processed my diagnosis and all its implications for myself, I could not open up about it. Now I felt ready – but how to broach the subject? Where to start?

Two books I had read about intelligent women who suffered from schizophrenia came to mind: *Welcome, Silence*, by Carol North, M.D. and *The Quiet Room*, by Lori Schiller and Amanda Bennett. They had been so accurate in their descriptions of what it is like to live with the disease. Their reflections resonated as if they were my own journal, had I kept one. So I decided that I would begin to reach out to my family with these books. I would be seeing my parents at my sister's graduation in a few weeks (motivation for me to indeed be discharged after my pass), and then again the end of June when they came out West to Vancouver.

I would give them my copies of the two books, I decided, and also copies of the quotes I had taken from them. They would then have both a general background as well as insight to my specific experience. My parents and I could then talk in June, and Kyla would be coming through Vancouver in August as she headed back to China.

Though I knew I had to try to explain my schizophrenia to my family, I also felt a burden to share my story with others: to my fellow schizophrenics, to their friends and their families, and to those who had nothing but an abstracted or confused idea of what the disease entails. To psychiatrists, psychologists, counsellors... I knew by now that so many of them had little idea of what living with schizophrenia was really like.

And to myself: I wanted to work at embodying my experience with words, and to have what I wrote be more than simply an intimate journal-writing exercise. A book, I decided. I would write a book that would be to others as *The Quiet Room* and *Welcome, Silence* had been to me. I wanted to draw alongside my fellow schizophrenics and let them identify with my experiences, and, most importantly, I wanted to give them hope and inspiration that even if you are at times psychotic you still have a life to live.

I wonder if all that mulling over stressed me that night. In any case, I was bordering on breaking. They wanted something from me. I tried placating Them with a binge and purge, but They were not appeased. I let Them give me suggestions on the writing of suicide notes and saw again the Deep Meaning in my own death. "Fuck off – I gave you enough already," I hissed. But They were insistent. *Blood, pain, blood, pain,* They insisted. I struggled against Them, reminding myself out loud that They weren't real, and the fact that if I were to slice my wrist or bang my head the nurses would insist my taking some rat-infested Ativan. *We want something from you.*

I remembered that, at VGH, They were pleased when I tried to take screws out to liberate people's souls that I psychotically believed were trapped underneath. Here at UBC, I had already heard their cries coming from the screws that held up light switch and electrical outlet plates. *Liberate seventeen,* I was instructed. I found a dime to act as a screwdriver, and set to work.

I had only five screws out when a nurse caught me. She asked for them, then demanded them when I refused. I tried to explain to her that this was a very benign way to satisfy Their demands, and that after I had let the seventeen souls out from behind their prison-screws I would replace the screws, no harm done. She didn't understand. She threatened injections of Ativan, the Quiet Room, and restraints. I tried and tried to get my point across but she refused to listen. I was becoming afraid by this point, terrified that she would not let me placate Them with soul liberation and that I'd therefore have to resort to something more harmful. *Please, please; I'll put them back after. Just please leave me to my task.*

I kept my five screws in my clenched fist. The nurse left, and I decided to hide in the bathroom; I had to change my tampon, anyway. So new tampon in hand I headed to the bathroom. I was intercepted by the nurse who now had with her the usual entourage.

"Give me the screws," a Security guard insisted. "You can't go about taking screws out. That's vandalism of hospital property."

"I'll put them back," I pleaded. "I just have to get seventeen. Please. I'm doing a good thing. If I take the screws out, I won't hurt myself like They are telling me to do."

Believing that the "people behind the screws" were

telling me to hurt myself, one said to me, "Just give us the screws. We're not going to put them back right away." I pondered this. As long as the screws were out, the people's souls could escape. It didn't matter who had them, as long as they were out. I could give them up now, avoid the Ativan and restraints, and get the other twelve I needed later.

"You're not going to put them back?"

"Nope."

"Alright." And I gave them over. Thinking that this scene was over, I turned back into my room.

"We're still going to need you to take this Ativan," the nurse said. She held out a med cup with the small white pills. The rat-bearing pills.

"No, I'm fine now. I'm calm. I don't need any Ativan."

"You have to take it. You choose: pills or an injection." I tensed. They weren't really going to do that, were they? I was fine. I just couldn't take the risk of getting rats in my brain.

"I can't take it. It has rats in it."

She stated the choice again, and then left. In my semi-deluded state I thought I had won. But then here were the nurses and guards again. The half-dragging, half-carrying to the Quiet Room; the holding, pinning down; the exposing of thigh and the cool alcohol swab; needle in, four milligrams of Ativan in, innumerable rats in. Through it all, I unconsciously still held my tampon in my hand. Cuff restraints, and it is wrenched from my clutch. Then, they were gone, a lone nurse left to keep watch for a few minutes until the chemical restraints kicked in.

"I need to go to the bathroom," I told the nurse. She sighed. I was already all tied up. "I brought something with

109

me," I prompted. She clued in.

"Do you absolutely have to? Can't it wait?"

"No." I had had the other one in eight hours already, and who knew how many hours they would have me in restraints.

"I'll have to do it for you, then," she answered. *What? She was going to…. No! Not that!* I was mortified.

"Noooooo. Please, no."

"But we can't have you messing up the bed," she said.

"NO! No! Please don't. Noooo." She had already left the room. A minute later, she came back with a pad.

"Erin, I'm going to put this on you." I pleaded with her to let me go to the bathroom, anything, just not that. My words became screams, but to no avail. My pyjama pants pulled down like a baby on a change table, she reached in, removed the tampon, and manoeuvred the pad into position. I cried. This can't be happening. Do they have no respect for a patient's dignity? I lay there sobbing at the pad, the restraints, the guards physically carrying me and pinning me down, the injection. *Noooo*, I sobbed. *No.*

And after all that, the guard had lied. The screws were back by the next day when I was out of restraints and able to check.

* * *

Apparently, I had been brought back to my bed sometime before noon that following day and had eaten meals. I believed her when my roommate, Elizabeth, told me so, but had no recollection of either. The whole day I was zombie-like, sleeping. I later learned that an injection of four milligrams of Ativan into a female of my size is an extreme dose. *Why*, I wondered. I had been trying to do something better than self-harm, and this is the result? It

110

made no sense. "This is the way, my dear Derrick boy," the Voices told me. "But no fucking way," They contradicted Themselves.

As I came out of my stupor, I began to realize that though the Tracker couldn't watch me in the hospital, someone – or something – was eyeing my every move. I saw shining red eyes staring at me from every wall of our room. Demon eyes! I had to cover those eyes; they were burning me with their intensity, and would surely hurt me after a suitable period of surveillance. They were all masquerading as power indicators on the electrical outlets of our room, but I knew what they really were. Demons. Devils. Legion, all through the ward, the hospital, the world. What could I use to cover those red, red eyes? Paper, certainly, as long as it was thick enough, would do. How to hold it there? No glue, no tape, no nails. Ah, I thought, as I became conscious of my rhythmic chewing. Gum!

Quickly, before Elizabeth returned or a nurse checked on me, I gummed the back of a piece of paper and stuck it to the plate. Too thin! The eyes, veiled but still visible, shone through. More paper, more gum; the silver-lined gum packaging was perfect! I worked almost frantically, chewing and sticking, afraid that I would be too late and the demon eyes would leap out at me and burn and devour and obliterate me.

"The watching demon eyes are now gone," I wrote on the paper coverings. The demon eyes were taken care of, but the next day I again saw the flying lights. *Purest points of light appear...* silver, white, and, unusually, black, too. I wasn't sure if they were angelic or demonic in origin, reward or punishment for covering the demon eyes. Cryptic Voices commented: "What of the hungry tonight? Virtuous, I see. And balls?"

111

Of great concern to me was the Tracker. I felt safe enough in the hospital and thought that he did not know where I was. But I knew that as soon as I returned home, he would begin to harass me again. I denied suicidality. If I wanted to die, I would just let the Tracker do it. Listening to the Voices were, I guess, a form of suicide ideation but if it got too dangerous, I would stop, yelling at the Voices: *"I don't want to die!"*

They had me see a psychologist during my stay. In conclusion, he made note that he found the test data "most consistent with the diagnosis of schizophrenia, of the paranoid subtype." In contrast to other doctors' opinions, he saw no indication of dysfunctional personality traits such as borderline personality disorder.

More interestingly, he made note that there was no "exaggeration of symptomatology" that would suggest I was magnifying my symptoms for support or other benefits. Benefits? Being tied to a stretcher for hours on end and being heavily medicated against my will could be benefits? That being yanked without warning from my cozy home and satisfying work was a plea for support?

When I was writing this chapter, I was also reading a memoir of someone who suffered from Munchhausen syndrome, a strange disorder in which an individual intentionally produces or feigns physical or psychological symptoms and demands medical treatment. The motivation is to assume the sick role. Was I doing that?

Do I really have schizophrenia? When well – i.e., on my meds – I seem so far removed from my schizophrenic symptoms. Did I truly believe that rats ate my brain and a Tracker sought to kill me? Or were they products of my abundant imagination? Were my Voices indeed Voices, or were They simply the voices everyone hears in their head?

I experimented. I tried to produce auditory hallucinations by thinking *really hard* but it was all in my head and was not self-sustaining. I thought back to my times of delusion and told myself those things were true but I didn't believe myself and there was no hint of the Deep Meaning to give it credibility.

Ever the scientist, I tried another experiment one day near the end of my hospitalization: could I replicate the actions, feelings, and thoughts of my psychosis? I therefore began slamming my head against the concrete wall in my room. Sure enough, staff rushed in and pulled me back. I resisted them, imitating what I recalled as "psychotic," and soon Security was called. I wrestled as usual, screaming and non-compliant, but soon bound. As Ativan was being drawn into the needle, I screamed for help to keep the rats out of me.

Behaviourally, it was a good show. It was familiar. But no matter how hard I tried, I could not feel what I was displaying. It all felt so forced, so alien, so false. I yelled about rats but did not believe myself.

Whenever I doubt my schizophrenia, I return to this experiment. Oddly, it reassures me.

Chapter 9: Romance and Brain Dialysis

By June of 2003, I was discharged, this time to the care of a UBC Student Health psychiatrist, Dr. Musly. Like Patti, my counsellor at Dalhousie, she was petite and motherly. In the medical treatment of my psychosis, however, she was aggressive. Soon I was again taking 1400 mg of Seroquel a day – much more than the recommended maximum of 800 mg. It was very sedating, but otherwise effective.

Richard, the Greek guy I had met during my last stay in PAU, and I had become friends in our sharing of candy and stories in the hospital. He had given me his phone number, so when I was out of the hospital, I got up the courage to call.

We were soon dating. I still didn't give much thought about whether or not I liked him; I was too obsessed with the fact that *someone* liked *me*. In retrospect, I see him as a player at best and an abuser at worst. But in that first year or two, he sweet-talked his way into my heart. I began to love him.

I was blind to the negatives that others saw in him. I saw them as simple personality quirks, as the emotionality of a true Greek. Having never before been in a serious and, importantly, sexual, relationship before, I attributed his somewhat abusive tendencies to *"men."* Moreover, I emphasized, to myself and to others, his consistent love and attention to schizophrenic, bulimic me. He visited me faithfully every time I ended up in the hospital. After a purge, I would crawl into bed with him, crying, as he pet my hair and told me that he loved me no matter what. I believed him. In December of 2003, we moved in together.

* * *

Before that, however, the Voices began speaking up again. Between my NSERC application for another two years of funding, paper preparation, seminar course, directed studies, and daily tasks at the lab, I was under a lot of stress. *Monday,* I kept reminding myself on Thursday. *It will be better by Monday.* Monday, besides being the usual day for a response paper for the seminar and the NSERC deadline, was when I wanted to submit my latest paper to an academic journal so as to be able to include it on my NSERC application. So after Monday, things would be a lot less stressful, I thought. And the Voices would go away, right?

With so much work to do, I eased up on my medication. I needed to be alert and able to concentrate; the amount of Seroquel I was on made me very drowsy and when I could, I slept at least 14 hours a night. But until Monday, I couldn't afford to be sedated. It wasn't quite a conscious decision. Each time it came to take my Seroquel, I simply estimated how much I could take and still perform to my high standards.

Friday morning I left for my usual appointment with Dr. Musly. I was distracted, the Voices harassing me relentlessly.

"Hi, Erin. How are you this week?" Dr. Musly greeted me.

She had dimmed the lights, a psychological experiment, I assumed. It reminded me of my talks with my old high-school friend, Marie, when we would begin talking in daylight, let it get dark with the setting sun, and not turn on the lights. Or sleepovers, when girl talk got more personal and revealing with increasing darkness. *Okay*, I thought. *Makes sense.*

She began talking, asking the usual questions. The Voices were bothersome, forbidding me to talk and I felt it was my duty to obey. She was the Enemy – why, I'm not sure. In any case, I said little.

Then I saw it. Across the room from me, Dr. Musly's filing cabinet had become inky black in the dim lighting. It looked infinite in its depth and then I realized what it was: a black hole. And there, in the middle, was a wooden handle. A handle – on a black hole? It could only mean that Dr. Musly "had a handle" on that black hole, that she understood it and, moreover, could manipulate and control it. And if she had a handle on such a complex and immense structure as a black hole, she must have a handle on the smaller, simpler brain in my head. She *was* the Enemy and anything I said would surely aid her handling of my brain. That must be avoided at all costs.

"Erin? Are you okay? What's going on?" She pressed me for answers, any communication. More direct questions I answered with an almost imperceptible nod or shake of my head. I dared not say more. I could imagine her pulling on the handle of my brain, opening it and disturbing the contents.

One way or another the appointment ended – early, thankfully – and I left. Voices and Their Deep Meaning swirled around me, but somehow I pushed Them aside as I concentrated on the work ahead of me that week.

*   *   *

"Do you prefer the lights bright, Erin?" Dr. Musly asked. I was back in her office for another session. Noticing something amiss in me Friday, she had insisted on a meeting first thing Monday morning.

I glanced at the filing cabinet.

"I like it green better," I answered.

"Green? The lights – do you want them dimmed like last time, or like this?" She hadn't understood my answer, but it seemed so laborious to explain it all.

"I like it green," I repeated.

She followed my gaze, and, noting the greenness of the cabinet, echoed, "Green." I gave a barely detectable nod. I was already on guard. Even though the black hole wasn't visible, I was wary.

The Voices were insistent, persistent. "She is not to be told anything," They warned. "Do not tell her, do not tell her, do not tell her...." I was unsure of what they were afraid that I would tell, so I said little on any subject. The Voices were so loud, I could barely follow the one-sided conversation. Then I heard it. The code word.

"... have a handle on things?" she was saying. Handle? *Handle*? Damn, she knew. She knew how she had a handle on a black hole and now she was going to reach out and grasp the handle of my mind and pull it out, all the files out. Files open, discarded, lost, scrambled, torn. She'd read them, add others of her own. My brain's sanctity would be breached and it terrified me. My only recourse was to give her no way to grasp that handle. I went mute.

"Erin? What's going on?" she kept asking. Her concern grew with my silence, realizing that I was, as she put it in her notes, "internally preoccupied." "Erin? Are you okay?" I was terrified. I retreated further into my world, the one controlled by the Deep Meaning and communicated by the Voices. They had been unkind to me in the past – and Dr. Musly had not – but still their power over me prevailed. I refused to speak, to communicate anything. *A handle.*

At a loss for what would reach me, Dr. Musly felt she had only one option. "I'm going to take you over to Emergency, Erin," she told me quietly. "Just to have you checked out by a doctor there."

I froze. Inwardly, that is; I had been physically motionless for a while already. Emergency? Hospital? No, not that. Not that again. I shook my head. "Yes, Erin. I'm sorry but I really have to." She left the room. I knew that she was going to talk to someone in Emergency about evaluating me, but I couldn't deal with that. I closed my eyes, visualizing the rest of my day – as I would have it. I would leave the appointment, catch the shuttle home, read my articles for my seminar, inject my mice, work on the paper, finish the NSERC application.... That was what was going to happen, I told myself. No hospitalization now. Not when I had it all planned out to be finished by today's deadline.

But no, I was wrong. I was going to Emergency, like it or not. Security was there, and fight as I may, the strong men always win.

"No! I'm not going to be hospitalized!"

"Yes, you are. You've been certified by a doctor." Firmly spoken by a nurse.

"No! You can't. You can't certify me – I'm not a danger to myself or to others," I spouted off, having learned by heart that admission phrase. But in fact I had been certified – "psychotic, paranoid and out of control" – and there was nothing I could do about it. Still I struggled, aggressive even, an unwilling patient labelled "aggressive/violent" with a "history of physical aggression" on the patient profile alert. So far from my normally peaceful, quiet, and respectful demeanour. In response to the question, "What do you understand is the reason for your admission?" it is written that I stated, "I don't need to be in hospital."

It is a big deal at the hospitals to which I've been admitted that patients be clad in hospital pyjamas, and it has to happen *right away* upon admission. Since I would be uncooperative, Security guards and nurses would wrestle me into them by force. Had I any emotional reserve left, I would have been extremely embarrassed of being stripped naked by a team of male Security guards. Looking back, it disturbs me.

This time, they got off all my clothes but my Care Bear undershirt. *Please leave me my Care Bear*, I pleaded. No, it was so important that I be stripped of my own clothes and jailed in the hospital's. I clung to it tightly.

"We'll just have to cut it off," one of them said. I panicked.

"No! Please! Don't cut my Care Bear, please. Please." Suddenly I was cooperative, taking the shirt off myself. Then my bra was taken off, and I was naked, bare. I struggled less as they put the blue pyjamas on me; I was cold and utterly shamed. They took away my glasses, even, lest I self-harm with them. For good measure, restraints were put on. I struggled; I was crying. I caught sight of my distressed face in the reflective metal of the bedside rails. Certified, hospitalized. Again.

* * *

They brought me by ambulance, in restraints, to

VGH. PAU again. The Enemies had their legal pads, pens, beepers. All the necessities to deal *professionally* with us crazies.

I kept mostly to myself ("bed seeking," as it is written in the nurses' notes). I was beginning to lose weight, I noticed, and this inspired me to retain my loss of appetite. I had weighed in at 131 pounds Friday morning, planning to lose one pound every two days in order to be back at 120 by the *Society for Neuroscience* conference I was going to at the end of October in San Diego. I was pleased as my stomach bulges shrank, my pelvic bones rising from their fatty sea. Oh, to be thin. This weight loss based on diminished eating was much better than the cycles of binging and vomiting I was used to. This anorexic fling was very satisfying. Could I keep it up until discharge? It was easy in the hospital to eat minimally from a tray.

One afternoon, they served up cheesy brains. I poked the tissue cautiously, disgusted. The menu proclaimed macaroni and cheese. Right. I knew better. "The brown spots, masquerading as macaroni ends, are really RATS so I didn't eat it," reads a little crayon picture I drew and titled later that day.

Then, they added a new torture: risperidone rats. The doctor had ordered risperidone in its liquid form, to be certain I was not cheeking my pills. I wasn't cheeking, and would cooperatively open my mouth to show the nurse I had swallowed the little pills; why, then, would they do this to me? Didn't they see that I was even refusing juice – water instead, please – to go with my handful of pills, lest there be rats there?

"I'm not taking it. There's rats in it," I said to the nurse when he brought me the little cup the first time.

"It's this way, or an injection," he countered.

"I can't. I already have too many rats in my brain," I pleaded. *Please, please, no more rats.* But of course, the injected medication went in, rats and all. After a few chaotic rounds of risperidone needles, the doctor finally had compassion for me and prescribed the drug in its tablet form.

To counter all the rats that they had been injecting into me, I had, at last, found a non-self-injurious way of ridding my brain of the dreaded rodents. I realized one day as I paced the circular ward that the walking lulled the rats. Like babies in their car seats, the rats slumbered in my head, becoming unable to resist the power of the aspirator. The aspirator was a pair of air vents in the ceiling of the ward, near the rooms facing 10th Avenue. Every time I passed by them, some of the sleepy rats were sucked up. Unfortunately, some brain matter was also aspirated, but the system was designed such that it was a sort of brain dialysis: it took up both brain and rats, but after filtering out the rats, the brains were returned to my head. It wasn't a perfect solution; it took several rounds to get any noticeable effect, and the smallest rats always passed through the filter and were returned, trapped in the neuronal matter.

So pacing the ward and subjecting myself to the aspiration and dialysis became an important part of each day. I was pleased that I had been shown this procedure (by the Deep Meaning, of course). Unlike the head banging, it would not ironically lead to an increase in the number of rats in my brain due to inevitable injections of Ativan. So I thought. It was something I assumed I would be allowed to do.

"Erin, I have some Ativan for you." What? "You seem agitated. You've been pacing the ward for ten minutes already. I want you to take this Ativan." Her pleasant demeanour soon turned angry and then the needle-wielding nurse and the strong Security men won.

*   *   *

Days spent on a psych ward are long, punctuated by the three trays of hospital food each day that rattled in their cage-like cart from food services. These highlights of the day were so anticipated that I would often think that *for sure* I was hearing the approaching cart, but, when I checked, there would be nothing yet. Given such anticipation you'd think that I would savour every bit of the measured portions they gave us, but it was rather an exercise in self-control. I would survey the contents of my tray and decide exactly what I would eat and how much. Most times it was the soup and vegetables only. Just enough, nothing extra. The nurses noticed but said little, leaving me to make the small amount of food I had decided to eat last as long as possible.

The self-discipline was fuelled by my continuing happiness – joy, even – of my slimming body. Every morning, and several times a day, I lay down on my bed and went through a routine examination: stomach first: was it flat? Visible pelvic bones? Legs raised perpendicular to my body, could I feel fat around the taut muscles? How much could I pinch on my arms? Were my ribs raised above their shallows as I ran my fingers over their tracks? Even my fingers: how loose were my rings?

Examinations complete, I had to fill the rest of the day. TV would have been an obvious choice, but I couldn't focus on it. Ironically, I could instead concentrate on more demanding tasks. I started a puzzle.

750 pieces later – no, 746: it was a public puzzle with missing pieces – I began another one. My world had shrunk

to little pieces, fully interlocking. Pictures emerged. Missing pieces, little gaps. Satisfaction was the click of a matching shape. I was alone in the task. No one was allowed to help. No one to mar my perfection.

I had brought in Care Bears and a blankie and these accompanied me to all puzzle sessions. In fact, they were with me at all times. Always they were either in my arms or propped up to watch me, their cute little faces smiling perpetually up at me.

"I wuv you, Ewin," they told me several times a day. "Ewin, I wuv you, I wuv you."

"I wuv you too," I cooed back at them and enveloped them in a tight embrace. I had three of my friends with me: a beanie Funshine Bear, and two – Share Bear and Wish Bear – "My First Care Bears" that were so soft. Aimed at infants, these Bears, when shook, rattled soothingly. I sometimes lay on my back, two Bears cuddled in my arms and one held up above my face. I grinned, happy. Their cute smiles and baby rattles made me all warm and fuzzy inside. They were my friends, my constant companions, my comfort. My Bears.

Many people suffering from schizophrenia display "disorganized" behaviour: unkempt hygiene, inappropriate behaviour, and agitation, for example. However, some professionals claim that other schizophrenics regress to child-like behaviour instead. This may explain why I showed little behavioural disorganization, except at my most ill moments, and instead clung to my Bears, my blankie, my colouring.

I rocked to soothe myself and at times sucked my thumb. My reaction to the threat of a PRN of Ativan is definitely reminiscent of a toddler in a tantrum: "No!" was given as a response to the choice of two alternatives (i.e.,

Ativan as a pill or an injection). Like a child, I thought I could dismiss it with defiance and denial. I had not known of this symptom of childishness at the time, but when I later read about it occurring in lieu of disorganized behaviour, I was comforted by this explanation.

"I brought you someone," Richard said one day. Slowly, he pulled a cuddly Bear from inside his jacket.

"Grumpy!" I took him into my arms. "Gwumpy Beaw! I wuv you," I greeted. He was freshly washed, white where he was once grey.

"I knew he was one of your favourites," Richard said. "I'd have brought him before but he hadn't dried out from his bath yet."

"I missed him," I confessed. "But I don't want him here. I've never seen Grumpy Bears in stores except when I bought him. He's too hard to replace if...." Not that anything would happen in there in the hospital. Still, I feared it.

"Okay, I'll bring him back. I brought you some candy, though, too. Jolly Ranchers, Big Red gum, Skittles."

"Just like last time," I commented. "Remember? We'd sit and talk and you'd share your candy with me when we first met here."

"Yeah. And there was that screamer girl that was always trying to steal it," he added. We smiled reminiscing.

"I really am scared about something happening to my Bears," I said, returning to that topic.

"Why?"

"Remember *her*?" I asked in a low voice, motioning towards Geri. He glanced over. During Richard's last visit, we had sat down on the couch in the common room together. A few minutes later, Geri lashed out at us.

"Get out of my seat!" Before we could react, she

continued. "You take mine, then I wreck yours." And with a swift movement of her pudgy hand, she grabbed a handful of my puzzle, wrenching the pieces from their places. "Ha," she said vengefully and wrecked another handful of my puzzle.

"Hey!" Richard rose from the couch. "Don't do that. We'll move." Noting that Geri had stopped the puzzle massacre, he strode off to the nurses' station. The nurse, knowing both my and Geri's personalities, quickly intervened by making Geri leave. Richard and I nonetheless gave up our seat on the couch lest we provoke further retribution.

"It's not so bad," Richard said of the puzzle damage. I looked at it, and saw that most of the pieces were still in clumps of attachment.

"I'll fix it later," I decided. "Thanks. I was kind of in shock when she yelled at us and attacked my puzzle before we could even say we'd move."

Geri had been ushered to her isolation room, and we finished our visit in peace. But that rash and mean action of hers made me fear her. If she wanted to get at me again, I knew that she would know to attack my Bears or blankie. So I kept them safely with me, and kissed Grumpy good-bye when he left with Richard.

*   *   *

My world had shrunk down to the size of the ward, and was much easier to deal with than all the stimulation and responsibility outside. Always, there was the fear of relapse. Part of me wanted out as soon as possible, but I was also scared. Could I *handle* things? Still, it wasn't long before I was discharged; things were, to a large extent quieter. Official diagnosis upon leaving: *chronic* schizophrenia. I guess six hospitalizations does that to your record. I knew what the chronicity meant: medications forever, high probability of relapse and subsequent hospitalization. It meant I was sick, the medications only holding things down.

Thursday, I gathered my things, got dressed in real clothes, and walked out. The sudden change jarred me, but I was soon home with Richard and in his arms. That night I cried. I cried for my lack of control over being certified, for the restraints and needles that hurt and humiliated me. Richard held me, soothing my sobbing and trembling. *I don't want to be sick,* I wept, *I don't want to be sick anymore.*

Chapter 10: Engaged!

I was turning 25 on the tenth of February, 2004. Richard and I had been together for almost a year, and we seemed to complement each other well. He was a true Greek, full of emotion and expression, while I was quiet, calm. He showered me with affection, both with caresses and words, and did not judge my schizophrenia or my bulimia. *I love you's* were abundant. I knew he would do something to make my birthday happy.

I, however, was irritable that day. Everything irked me and, after a long day at the lab, all I wanted to do was crawl into bed and sleep. Maybe it was remembering the birthdays I'd spent in hospitals, maybe it was turning a significant number when I felt that I'd accomplished much less than I had hoped due to my many hospitalizations and medications. In any case, it was not a happy birthday.

The next day was different. I was in a better mood, cheerful. After work and supper, Richard and I were watching a (lame) reality show. The contestants were choosing teams: "I choose Lisa." "I choose Ben." "I choose Malcolm." Then, all of a sudden, Richard was down on one knee in front of me, saying, "Erin, I choose you. Will you marry me?" He held up a ring in its little box.

"Yes, yes, a thousand times yes!" I exclaimed. He slid the ring onto my finger. I was engaged!

I wanted to tell my parents first, but, because of the four-hour time difference between Vancouver and New Brunswick, had to wait until the next day. I had to go in to the lab and tried to hide the hand my ring was on. Nevertheless, Melissa saw it almost as soon as I arrived. "Is that what I think it is?" she asked excitedly.

"Yes! Richard proposed last night!"

"I'm so happy for you!" Then, as women are wont to do, exclaimed, "Let me see the ring!"

I was able to keep my secret from everyone else and excitedly called my parents that afternoon. They were happy too, though they hardly knew Richard. They trusted my judgement.

It took a few weeks to settle on a date. Richard was in less of a hurry than I was, though we agreed on a summer wedding. We finally decided on the second Saturday in July of the next year, 2005. Now to plan what would really be a "big, fat" Greek wedding. In July of 2004, we attended his sister's "big, fat" Greek wedding where I met Richard's extended family and large circle of friends. In the year to come, his sister, Rosa, would prove both very helpful with the wedding planning but also determined to have my wedding the way *she* wanted. But no matter now – I was engaged!

Chapter 11: Play-Dough and Care Bears

Planning a wedding is stressful, and hints of my psychosis were emerging. First to fall by the wayside was taking my medications as prescribed; by November of 2004, I was only taking 300 mg of Seroquel. "Decompensation due to medication non-compliance" is a very common experience among people with schizophrenia. We feel fine, normal even, and no matter the commitment to health (e.g., promised drug adherence at the end of a stay in the hospital) there is so often another downfall, another hospitalization. After nearly a year stabilized on my Seroquel, I, spurred on by returning Voices, thought I could taper down the amount I was taking. Inevitably, it meant that I was headed towards hospitalization number seven.

*   *   *

Tuesday, I left for my seminar as usual. I had sent in my review paper the day before, but it had been a challenge to get it done. It was just so hard to *think* these days. I couldn't concentrate, couldn't focus my attention. My memory, too, was failing me. Over and over again, I would lose track of the topic of conversation after each statement. Richard would say something, and as I opened my mouth to answer, I would have no clue as to what he had said. I was losing moorings, adrift in a sea of disjointed conversations and lost thoughts. More than it was frustrating, it was scary.

It followed me to my seminar. Moreover, the Voices came too. I sat in the back, trying hard to follow the discussion. But not only was my memory betraying me and my Voices distracting me, my brain was slowly being filled with play-dough. It was the work of the Deep Meaning, I knew, and the Voices didn't make things any easier. Every effort to think was thwarted by the dense dough. Then, to further hinder me, They added some yeast. The play-dough in my brain leavened, filling every convolution. I tried to mentally punch it down, but with no success.

Only the Voices could penetrate the mass, hounding me relentlessly. "Hey, look how stupid she is! Dumb, dumb, dumb. Can't she even follow what that student is saying? SO stupid, that girl. You, you, you – you're the stupid one!" and They laughed. I wanted to cry. The yeast-filled play-dough rose and suffocated me. Class ended and I fled.

I spent most of the week at home. I dreaded the thought of going to work, of having to uphold a semblance of normalcy for so long and for so many people. I really tried to be working during my days at home, but with little success. It was almost all I could do to get ready for next week's seminar. Reading was made impossible by the yeasty play-dough and words would not come for my essay. It was so discouraging, but I was determined to work and thus prove that I was not becoming ill.

* * *

I had an appointment Friday morning. Dr. Musly wanted me to take my medication, of course. The Seroquel I decided I could handle, but I balked at the risperidone she

130

was insisting on. I just didn't quite trust it. I feared that, even in its pill form, it contained rats, existing in a sort of freeze-dried state. She was adamant, though.

"Just 1 mg at night, Erin," she told me. "Will you take it?"

"No," I replied, softly but firmly. I was taking no chances, giving not the slightest possibility for the rats to infiltrate my system again.

Slightly exasperated, Dr. Musly said, "You need to take the risperidone, Erin. It's a low dose. You're just not doing well right now and I think that taking the risperidone will make things easier to handle." *Handle*? The code word again. What did this mean? While I tried to figure this out, she left the room to fetch some sample boxes of risperidone.

"And I want you to take one right now, Erin." She popped a pill out of its enclosure and handed it to me. It was one of those dissolving tablets, disintegrating as soon as it touched my tongue. I was afraid. Dr. Musly looked at me a moment, and then I saw her expression change. "You're not going to throw it up when you leave here, are you?"

"No." I sighed.

"I hope not. Now, I want you to come in for an appointment on Monday." She flipped open her little electronic planner, slotted me in. A little pink slip reminder for me. "And Erin, if you're not doing better by then, we may have to consider hospitalization again. I don't want to have it come to that, but you really aren't well, Erin."

I left, numb. Surely it couldn't end with another hospitalization, could it? I knew Dr. Musly would follow through with it if she thought it was really necessary, whether or not *I* thought it was needed. I felt hopeless. I went home.

I wasn't convinced I might need to be hospitalized but I did know that Dr. Musly was capable of certifying me. I felt resigned to that certain fate now. At least I could be prepared, for once, I thought. Carefully, I packed two small bags: toiletries, underwear and socks, a book, crosswords, colouring books and Crayolas. *Care Bear* colouring books, that is, since colouring in Care Bear books was a favourite activity of mine in the hospital. The pictures were almost sickly-happy, filled with hearts, stars, flowers, and rainbows. The Bears roller-skated along the rainbow trails and swung on swings hanging from stars. For the most part, I coloured them according to their "real" colours, but not always. Sometimes, I just wanted to use other colours. Oh, such rebellion. When in the hospital, first thing in the morning and last thing at night, I coloured. Of course, I also had to have my Care Bear blankie and three Bears. I chose them carefully: a middle-sized Funshine Bear that fit just right tucked into my arm when I slept, a beanie Cheer Bear – well loved, losing stuffing, and hair matting – and baby rattle Wish Bear.

In some part of my brain I hoped that by packing the bags I was jinxing the possibility of being hospitalized. I hid the bags from Richard, feeling guilty, hiding, but the belief that if I told no one then it couldn't be really true prevailed. That weekend, I simply withdrew from life, citing stress as the source.

"I'll go with you, then," Richard offered when I told him on Sunday night about Monday's appointment; he wanted to talk some sense into my hospitalization-happy psychiatrist.

"Thanks," I answered, but inside I felt uneasy. Deep down, I knew that something wasn't quite as right as it had been at other times in the past. I felt vulnerable and weak.

132

The Voices were bothering me again, and it was just so hard to *think*. Yeasty play-dough still fazed me and my working memory continued to decay.

I was not going to let Them win. I would show Dr. Musly that I was okay. I'd work all weekend; a psychotic schizophrenic couldn't accomplish that, I reasoned, so if I could do it, it would mean that I was not sick. That was what I told myself, tried to convince myself of. So I worked.

My main task was my upcoming presentation for the seminar. I had read the required papers and now had only to put their contents into a PowerPoint presentation. That was easy, requiring little real thought. I enjoyed making slides just so, getting the points across with eye-pleasing layouts. I didn't go overboard with animations and that stuff; basic, but with a little extra effort to style. I liked developing ways of presenting data and ideas with pictures and charts, condensing and clarifying.

This was my project for the weekend and I gave it my full effort. I pushed past the Voices, struggled against the play-dough. I would show Them! By Sunday night, I had a solid presentation ready and was confidant that this would prevent Dr. Musly from hospitalizing me. Surely I wasn't sick if I could accomplish what I had, right?

Monday morning, I left for the appointment that I now felt was unnecessary. So what if I hadn't taken the risperidone; I didn't need it. I had proved that. Richard had still been wanting to come, but he had been unable to get to sleep until the early morning and so I left him sleeping while I went alone. That was better, I figured, anyway. Although I was convinced that I did not need to be hospitalized, I knew by now that it was not necessarily my decision to make and Dr. Musly could certainly certify me if she wanted. I did not want Richard to witness my entering hospital, if that was what it came to. It was never a pretty sight.

"The Enemy, she's the Enemy," the Voices reminded me as I sat down in Dr. Musly's office Monday morning. "Don't tell her anything. Nothing."

"Erin? How was the weekend?"

I wanted to tell her about my productivity, my proof of sanity and health. But whispers of "...*Enemy*..." silenced me.

"Did you at least take the risperidone?" she continued. She looked doubtful. I shook my head, confirming the doubt.

I don't remember how much more we talked, or rather, she talked and I sat silently. At some point, she left the room and I could hear her talking outside. Security was called, the UBC Emergency doctor notified. Incoming paranoid schizophrenic. Incoming *resistant* schizophrenic.

It played out almost exactly as the last admission. The strong men won the battle of dragging me to Emergency's isolation room.

I was stripped of street clothes. Again.

Hospital pj's. Again.

Rat-releasing crashes of my head into the concrete. Again.

Held down.

Restrained.

Crying.

Pleading.

Needles.

Rats.

Terror.

Screams.

Again.

*   *   *

Days blurred together. I took my meals on my bed, privately determining how much to let into my body. Puzzles – 500, 750, and then 1000 pieces – kept my attention focused on a place far from where I was. Richard brought my pre-packed bags in for me. I cuddled my Bears as I coloured alone in my room.

One strong comfort was hidden in my box of Crayola crayons: a straight-edged razor blade, purchased from a Dollar Store way back when I was in the NS hospital in Nova Scotia, was brought out of hiding and used for bloody relief. I hunched myself under my blanket, hidden from the ever-watching camera. (Though "odd and suspicious behaviour" was noted in my charts and my pretence of sleep whenever the nurse would come in only confirmed this for them – but they never questioned me on it.) I drew the sharp blade across my skin. Drops of deep red appeared and slid down my arm. As before, I cut on my upper arms so as to hide it from any nurse taking my blood pressure. Criss-crossed lines marked my pale skin and I sopped up the blood with paper towel from the bathroom. The familiar peace flowed into me as my blood flowed out. I hid the blade in the crayon box again for next time. I smiled.

It had been a long time since I'd last cut. I'm not quite sure what moved me to plant the razor in the bags I knew Richard would bring in, and to hide it successfully from the inspecting nurses. I used it thankfully, secretly, daily. My old, whitened scars were laced with new red ones, forever a reminder of those moments .

"We're going to move you over to the open ward," a nurse greeted me one morning. I had spent almost a week in the cells but was then quickly moved. Almost immediately, I began my circular pacing.

135

Round and round the patient goes, what she does nobody knows. I got the usual curious stares from fellow patients. *Round and round, round and round, like the wheels on the bus.* I passed by the aspirator several times, but no rats and brain were sucked up. Were the rats not lulled yet? Were they resisting the process? Had any rats left over from the last hospitalization told the new ones of the aspirator? I walked faster. It wasn't working. I passed under the vents again but it was futile. It was too thick! The aspirator couldn't work on my yeasty play-dough brain. I started to panic. My head – open the wounds and let the blood release them. No choice. Bears held tightly, I wedged myself into a corner. Thud. Thud. Again and again, over and over. *Please, release me from the torment of the rats,* I pleaded. Thud. Thud. Thud.

A patient hears me, sees me. Nurses appear, pulling me away from my release. *No, no, let me go. The rats, the rats! No, no, no. Please, no. I need to get them out, the aspirator's not working, my brain is play-dough, yeast clogs the aspirator, and I must bleed.* A bloody circle on the wall stares back at me.

* * *

Earlier that day, Madeline, a girl I had met at the eating disorders support group on campus I attended, was, by coincidence, on her psych rotation for her nursing studies that week. I had bumped into her earlier while I circled the ward. She had noticed me, but since the nurses had still not given me my glasses, I couldn't see who she was until I was close by.

"Erin, hi," she said as she intercepted my rounds.

"Oh, hi, Madeline. You're here for your nursing practicum," I spouted bluntly, remembering.

"Yeah. But it's professional, you know; I'm not supposed to talk to you."

"That makes sense."

"I know. But I can see you when I'm done tonight," she said.

"Sounds good." I looked down at the three Bears in my arms. "I like Care Bears," I stated. Madeline smiled at me and my Bears.

"I'll see you later, Erin."

Later, when she stopped by to visit with me, I was in my old cell-room waking up groggy and in restraints because of the earlier head-banging. Sensitive to my dignity – rather, my lack of dignity – in those restraints, she stood at the nurses' counter, writing. A nurse brought the note in:

"Hi Erin,

"I would love to come and talk with you, but because of my role here (professional), I have been advised not to. But, I _can_ come and visit you/talk to you on the phone, if you want me to, in the context of your friend. I'm here right now, Don will read this to you. If you want me to come in, I'd be happy to. If you don't want to see me right now, please call me when you want." She signed it with her phone number._

"Yes," I told Don after I had read it through. "I want to see her." He went out and Madeline came in. "Hi, Madeline."

"Oh, Erin," she said sympathetically. I looked up at her as I lay held down by the restraints. I had thought that I would be embarrassed, but it was simply "this is the way it is." One of the nurses, kind despite her duty to restrain me, had placed my Care Bears beside me, softening the situation. Madeline and I talked a few minutes and she held my hand. I felt her kindness and sensitivity and was thankful.

"Your Care Bear is cute," she said. "I used to have Cheer Bear."

"I have a lot," I admitted. "Want to hear a funny story?"

"Sure."

* * *

"Well, I dreamt about Care Bears again," I told Richard one morning. "I don't really remember it very much, but this is the third night in a row that I've dreamt about them."

"Hmmm."

I left it at that, but I could sense something Meaningful welling up. It was of the Deep Meaning, I could tell, and remembered from past experience that only I could apprehend the Deep Meaning. It would be pointless to try and convey this message to Richard, or anyone else.

Small but persistent Voices swirled in and around my brain. "Come get us, Erin. Erin, we need you! Come, Erin, come!" With every passing day, these pleas became louder, stronger, more insistent. It was the Care Bears, I knew. They were calling me to them, that much was clear. But where were they? I was certain that the mutant Care Bears at the Toys R Us – the ones with hard bellies that, when pressed, lit up and emitted a mechanical voice – weren't the ones.

Thus began the search; a quest, really. I was drawn by the Voices and driven by the ever-increasing sense of urgency and Meaning. "Where are you?" I pleaded with them.

No answer to that question. "Come rescue us, Erin," was all they would say. Okay, so think rationally: what stores are most likely to sell Care Bears? Toys R Us was the most obvious one. "To… Toys… Toys R US," I muttered to myself as I scanned the telephone directory. "Locations: Broadway – yes, checked there." Richmond? Willowbrook? Even Surrey. Would I really have to travel that far to get them?

The Care Bears kept calling for me, filling my head with their Voices. At least these Voices were cute and child-like. They were insistent, yes, but not harsh or mean. So Friday night I left Richard playing video games with his friend, Kirk, headed to Metrotown, greater Vancouver's largest shopping centre. I was in luck – a Toys R Us. Heart fluttering with anticipation I looked up and down the aisles until –

"You're here!" I exclaimed.

"Erin! Erin! You found us! Erin!"

"Oh, you guys! I'm so happy – I found you. You were calling, and –"

"Erin!"

So there I was, talking out loud to some little stuffed toys. There were the regular size Care Bears, but I ignored them. I knew that it had been the little ones that had been calling me. The Voices had been juvenile, high-pitched, and simple in their wants and vocabulary. And they didn't chide me for taking so long in finding them, as an adult Care Bear might have.

The little Care Bears jostled around on their shelf. There were eight different ones – Bedtime Bear, Funshine Bear, Cheer Bear... "I'm here, you guys! But I can't take all of you." They agreed that I didn't need to buy more than one of each kind, but were shocked when I began choosing which few I would buy.

"Erin, we all need you," said Friend Bear.

"I'm sorry, guys." I lined them up on the shelf. Okay, my three favourites... Wish Bear, Share Bear, and Friend Bear. I headed for the cash.

"Erin, Erin, don't leave us! Erin...." they wailed, the ones on the shelf being joined by the ones in my arms. I had to go back.

"Okay guys. I'll take Funshine Bear and Bedtime Bear. But I already have a pink Love-A-Lot, so not little Love-A-Lot or Cheer Bear. And I don't really like the green on Good Luck Bear, so you three I really can't take. Sorry, but you little guys cost

money." I made it through the cash this time (the cashier gave me a smile as she scanned my little family through). I left the store, headed up on the escalator.

"Erin! Come get us, please, please pretty please. Erin, don't let us down!" And inside my book bag, the five I had chosen squirmed around and chimed in. "We need the other three, Erin. We're a family."

By this time, I knew that if I left those three there that they would call me, and the others would plead with me, until I returned for them.

"Yay! Erin's coming!" I turned down their aisle and couldn't keep a grin from spreading across my face.

"I'm sorry, guys. You're right. You all belong with me." Cheer Bear and Good Luck Bear practically leapt into my arms. "But do you really need to come, Love-A-Lot?" I asked. "I already have big Love-A-Lot." She looked at me, almost in tears.

"Erin, you wouldn't really leave me here all alone, would you?"

I couldn't. So three more Bears were added to the five in my bag. My own little octuplet family, Bears that had chosen me, called me, and had waited somewhat patiently until I had found them. I lined them up on my lap on the SkyTrain. "You're safe with me now, little guys."

"... and here I am worrying about you, and you show up with fucking Care Bears?" Richard burst out when I got back and was pulling Care Bear after Care Bear from my bag. I guess I hadn't communicated to Richard that I was going to be gone a couple hours, not just a walk around the neighbourhood. But a miscommunication is soon forgiven, and he left me to my Care Bears like I left him to his video games. I lined them all up with me in bed and played and talked with them. They became cherished toys to me, making me smile that the Deep Meaning could sometimes do something happy.

Madeline grinned carefully at my story, but soon had to leave. I later told it to some other friends. For once I could happily share and laugh about something schizophrenic. Driving me home once, Daniel, the Master's student I worked with, brought it up. "You have changed a lot over this past year, Erin," he said. "And how you're so open about your schizophrenia, and able to see the humour in it – that's so healthy. You just take it, like, that's life, and go through it."

"I – well, thanks. That means something to me." It did. I wanted so much to be more socially normal. Not in wishing my schizophrenia away, but, with the priceless aid of anti-psychotics, of connecting with other people and being free to laugh or cry about what life dishes out to each one. Finding an equality: I have funny stories to tell, just like you do. Doesn't matter anymore if they stem from hallucinations and delusions; I told a funny story, and people laughed. Simple, but for a schizophrenic just learning what social interaction is, that is enough.

*   *   *

I was still in the hospital.

After another week or so, things had quieted down. For me, though, it wasn't that the rats were gone; I simply could no longer detect them. The Voices still punctuated my days and nights with absurd comments, but, for the most part, I could effectively ignore them. I was deemed well enough to be transferred to an inpatient ward.

My bed was in a room of four, beside the window. "Leave your things here and I'll show you around the ward," the nurse said. Then she wanted to weigh me.

I was nervous as she led me towards the scale. I had been "good" while on PAU, eating little. (The staff was

141

aware of this. "Ate minimally" is sprinkled throughout my charts. They thought I was paranoid that the food was filled with rats.) I knew I had lost weight, but would the scale offer a number that I would be able to accept? I would have been confidant at home, on my own scale, but it was the only scale I trusted. How close would this scale be to mine?

I took off my shoes. "Fifty... fifty five and... six tenths," she read in kilograms. I quickly did the math: 122, 123 pounds. Good enough. I passed my hand over my flat stomach as I stepped off. There was still that ever-present small bulge just below my waist, but otherwise I was pleased. I was even more pleased when I read in my intake notes that my physical appearance was said to be "slender, petite."

* * *

Soon, I regained my appetite. Snacks were put out twice a day here, with name stickers identifying what each patient got. I received the same dairy products each time: a chocolate milk, a yoghourt, and cheese and crackers. Unlabelled muffins were available to all. Yummy. I hadn't had snacks for over a week. Surely I could indulge a bit in these healthy ones?

Indulge I did, and I felt too full. A trip to the bathroom, quietly purging the offending foods. I had forgotten how good it felt to empty my stomach, the rush of adrenaline and the feeling of being cleansed. So it happened again after the next snack. And the next.

Within a couple of days the snack binging and purging wasn't enough. In addition to my snacks, I checked last meal's trays for leftovers and helped myself to the always-available bread and butter. More in, more out.

What really tipped me over the edge into the bulimia again was being given privileges. I was allowed an hour out, unaccompanied, provided I remained on hospital grounds. To me, that meant I could binge at the hospital cafeteria and coffee shop, as well as take advantage of the various vending machines. Every day, I planned carefully: eat my suppertime meal – all of it – snatch some leftovers, consume any food I had saved from afternoon snacks, and then take my pass. I had an hour to get as much food in as possible and then to vomit it out. This occurred in a hospital bathroom that was hardly used during the evening, and I went back to my ward feeling refreshed and cleansed.

I thought that this routine was controlled. But letting just a "controlled" amount of bulimia in never ends there. Parasitic and devouring, it began to take over. Snacks, meals, treats Richard brought. I was soon throwing up three to five or more times a day. I had lost any control I thought I had. Boredom and powerlessness pushed me further into the bulimia. I told myself the old and useless promise that it would be context-specific; that when I left the hospital, it would not follow. So, dulled by that thought, I ate and vomited again and again.

*　*　*

Melissa was wanting to come by and visit. Up till now, I had not wanted any visitors other than Richard. I didn't want to be reminded of life outside psych wards and of how I was called sick. Melissa did come for a short time one evening, but that was all I could *handle.*

I was on 2 West for just over a week when I was put on discharge planning. I acknowledged to staff that "no rats = go home" as they put in in my chart. I wanted desperately to leave, but I was so scared to rejoin the "outside" world. I went an overnight pass and a few day passes; all went smoothly. So Thursday afternoon, I packed my bags and left.

I had left, but the illness and all its repercussions had not left me. They followed, enveloping me in a haze of self-doubt, depression, and hopelessness. Of all my seven hospitalizations, this one had taken the most out of me, away from me. After every hospitalization before, I had vowed never to return, but this time that promise would not come. I had been cut out of life again, cheated of normalcy. I had a sickness that would not be healed and I hated it.

I returned to work; tried to, at least. I dreaded every day of being around "normal people." I hated the leftover Voices that made inappropriate comments and the fear of returning rats. I could not function mentally very well either. Memory, concentration, attention… every mental task was difficult and demanding, some near impossible. Those were the primary deficits. Secondary to those problems were the emotional deadness and apathy about life. Combined, they prevented me from functioning. I took day after day off, not even able to work at home. Nothing helped. I was sick with scizophrenia's negative symptoms.

I had never had much insight into the fact that most schizophrenics experience significant and debilitating cognitive deficits. Anti-psychotic medication, even if it effectively controls the psychotic symptoms, generally does little to attenuate the cognitive problems. Moreover, these difficulties tend to increase over time. A vision of a presenter's slide from a schizophrenia talk plagued me: a downward slope of cognitive decline, punctuated with bouts of psychosis. That was refractory schizophrenia. That, they said, was me.

I began to really question myself. Here I was attempting to complete a graduate degree in Neuroscience while plagued by refractory schizophrenia. How realistic was that? It had taken me five and a half years to finish my BSc, and I was already two and a half years into my Master's. Would I ever finish the doctorate I so wanted? I doubted it.

Realistic: that's what I had to be. I dealt first with the problems at hand. I dropped my seminar course and extended the Directed Studies I was pursuing in another Neuroscience lab under Dr. Lewisson, a professor studying schizophrenia. Not having my electives done by December meant that it would be virtually impossible to effect my plan of switching from the Master's directly into the PhD. Maybe, due to my medical issues, they could make exception, but only maybe. I thought about it.

I thought also about Andrew's lab. I was unhappy with Andrew as a supervisor. He knew little of my day-to-day work and was of even less use when problems arose. When we had been emailing before I came to the lab, he had endless ideas that sounded exciting, but, as I found out when I came to the lab, were often unrealistic. It seemed increasingly unlikely that I would be able to pursue the projects I had initially outlined.

All these points swirled around inside me until one day everything aligned: a moment of eclipse. I would leave the lab. I would wrap up my work and complete it as a Master's degree and find a new lab for my PhD. A timeline became clear: I would tidy up loose ends, and begin writing up my thesis. If I defended it in May of 2005, I would be able to focus on wedding plans unfettered. A Vancouver marriage in July, reception and honeymoon in New Brunswick to follow, and I'd be ready to start fresh by the end of August. It seemed the obvious choice to make, and so I made it.

Telling Andrew was hard. It seemed so out of the blue to him. The usually ever-talking man was overly quiet as I explained myself to him. He had been counting on me to do a PhD in his lab, as had been my plan until now.

I knew what my first choice was for a lab to do my PhD in: Dr. Lewisson's. I was impressed with his character and science. More importantly, I finally felt ready to do schizophrenia research. It was where my passion lay now; at the *Society for Neuroscience* conference I attended in San Diego, I was drawn more to the schizophrenia posters than to those relating to my work in Andrew's lab. I trembled a little as I knocked on Dr. Lewisson's door.

"Come in, Erin," he greeted. "Have a seat." I sat. "Are you feeling better?" He had known that I had been in the hospital.

"Sort of," I answered noncommittally. I swallowed, nervous. "As you know, I had been planning to switch from the Master's into a PhD in Andrew's lab," I began, "but I have decided to finish up the Master's and start the PhD in another lab afterwards and I was wondering, um, if I could do it in your lab?" My voice rose into a question mark.

He sat back in his chair. "Hmmm." I waited. "It might work. Let's see… I'm just thinking about the space. I have two post-docs coming in January. Hmmm." He mentally evaluated my request.

"I can't say right now," he concluded. "I'll have to talk it over with the post-docs. They'd be the ones working with you. But," he said as he rose and walked to a table, pulled two files out, and handed them to me. "This is a grant proposal we're sending out this week and the other is a paper we just got accepted. Copy these and look them over to get a better sense of what we do in this lab."

I nodded, taking the papers. I still had something to

say. He sat back down. "I feel that there's something I should tell you," I began. My palms were sweating. "My interest in schizophrenia research is personal... I myself have been diagnosed with schizophrenia. That's why I was in the hospital. It means I can't always do as well as others; it means I may suddenly be hospitalized and unable to work for a time."

He took it in. "Thank you for telling me, Erin. That was very brave of you." Brave? Telling was just something I felt I should do, being up-front about a condition that could detract from my productivity. But yes, it had felt like it had taken some courage to actually say the words. I had disassociated during those few sentences, feeling like a parrot repeating what I had heard psychiatrists say over and over again.

Dr. Lewisson accepted me into his lab. I would begin doctoral work in September of 2005, assuming my thesis defence went well and I could receive my Master's degree. I threw myself into my work.

*   *   *

However, the next month or so was really difficult. I avoided people as much as possible, in person or on the phone, which meant as little time in the lab as possible. My patience was thin and expired well before 5:00 quitting time, so I left. No explanation, no excuse; I just went home. I did try to work once home, but I couldn't focus. My mood slipped lower, motivation following suit. I didn't care. Voices whispered around my head. "Lazy thing, that girl. Lazier than lazy. See her just lie there. Laaa-zy." And I hate laziness. I tried to force it, but I couldn't. I just *couldn't*. All I saw was that line of declining function from that chart. I was fated to slide down, down, down. to hopelessness.

Feeling hopeless leads me to overeat. I ate

147

compulsively, vomiting some but not all of my indulgences. Pounds were added and I crept up to 132 pounds. Too much, but I didn't much care. It had begun on the inpatient ward with my constant binging and purging. I had thought and hoped that it would not transfer with me outside the hospital, but I had been wrong. It flared up worse than it had been in over a year. Had I made any progress last year, I wondered, if here I was back to a life of bulimia? Richard, too, was discouraged. Would it ever be better?

As if I wasn't already having problems getting to work, the bulimia made it even worse. Binging and purging take time, and that time was often stolen from the working hours. It was a vicious compulsion from which I couldn't break free. It consumed me more and more as I myself consumed the food. One cycle wouldn't satisfy me; I did two, three, even four in a row. No relief. Increasing pain, relentless despair. Thoughts of suicide punctuated my mind. *Step in front of that bus, Erin,* I told myself. *Cut again, deep. Pills, ropes….it doesn't matter how.* I didn't have the energy to do anything, though. *Maybe I'll be lucky and my bulimia will kill me.* Or I thought of the Tracker. Sometimes, I'd open the curtains wide and stand in front of the window, inviting him to shoot me.

"Maybe we should try an antidepressant," Dr. Musly suggested one Friday. Somehow, she got me to talk every week and knew most of what was going on. I was against the addition of an antidepressant to my medication. Receiving one type of medication was enough for me, and I couldn't accept a second. It was even difficult taking the risperidone in addition to the Seroquel.

That risperidone was up and down, and probably contributed to my low mood throughout November and December of 2004. The psychiatrist in the hospital had taken me off the risperidone at my request, but he was the only psychiatrist to hold that opinion. Dr. Musly was particularly adamant that I be taking it.

"It will clear your mind, make it easier to think," she told me on several occasions. I was off it at first, then up to 2 mg... 2 mg... down again to 1 mg, 0.5 mg... back up to 2, down to 1 mg and back. A risperidone roller coaster. Maybe that contributed to my moods and motivation? At 2 mg, I was clearer in the mind but more tired. 1 mg did little in either direction. And at all levels, those tiny pills made me constantly hungry.

Being constantly hungry is hard enough, but here I was bulimic at the same time. I ate, I vomited, I gained weight. I hated it, but not with enough force to stop it. So I ate some more, vomited some more, and gained some more weight.

Still, despite my depressed mood and lack of care, I managed to get myself to my weekly appointments with Dr. Musly and to Wednesday's eating disorder group meetings. I managed some work, some productivity. I felt the tug of hopelessness and the invitation my illness gave to just let it all go. Dr. Musly had offered to write me a note, excusing me from work for a period of time. I looked at that option, but I was determined not to let schizophrenia win over my life. It may hospitalize and demoralize me at times, may snatch away measures of my valued cognitive function, may even take my dreams away. I may never finish my PhD. I may be warned not to have children while on medication and be told that it is too dangerous for my own health to be off it for nine months. I don't know what schizophrenia will take from me. But I do know that I will not give it things it does not take.

"I'm a survivor,
I'm not gonna give up,
I'm not gonna stop,
I'm gonna work harder.
I'm a survivor,
I'm gonna make it,
I'm a survivor,
Keep on surviving."
                        - Destiny's Child

I played this song over and over. In my iTunes playlist, it is followed by *"There's a Hole in the World"* by the Eagles. Its a sad tune and the lyrics tug at my heart. It often feels like schizophrenia is a hole in my world. *A cloud of fear and sorrow.* Its answer? *Don't let there be a hole in the world tomorrow.* Don't give it what it does not take.

Chapter 12: Dying Time, Again

One Monday morning in late January of 2005, I withdrew to my safe hideaway on UBC campus: an old phone closet. Crammed into the small space, I watched through the door cracks as legions of miniscule rats marched past me along the corridor. They were armed with lasers – lasers with which they could force entry into my body. I prayed they wouldn't see me.

There seemed to be no end to the rats, and I could not remain cramped long enough to wait them out. I had to go. Terrified, I stepped out of hiding, into the swarms of laser-wielding rats. Pinpricks pierced my skin and I ran to escape the assault. So many, successful, infiltrated my body. *No, not more rats, no.* I reached the end of the corridor and bolted through the door. Pulling it closed behind me, I thankfully realized that the rats did not come through with me.

I needed another safe space, an escape from the visual and tactile hallucinations of those lasering rats. I followed a set of stairs at the UBC hospital up to the end, above the top floor. No one would come by here, I thought. Alone, I hunched into the corner. My head rested on the cold concrete of the wall and I ached for the calming rhythm and dulled pain of striking my head. More importantly, it would bleed out any of the laser-rats that had managed to penetrate my body. I pulled back, thrust forward, again and again. Skin broken, bloody patches grew on the dirty concrete, bleeding out the rats. Over and over, I engaged in my comforting assault. Voices encouraged me.

I had thought I would have privacy there in the stairwell. Before too long, however, I heard steps approaching. I thrust harder, desperate to continue in my ritual. The footsteps approached, then faded as they passed me and went on. Or had I imagined it all? The steps that echoed in the stairwell – were they hallucination? No matter. I was free to continue my bloody banging. Had to get those rats out that lasered into me earlier.

The next footsteps were not imagined. "Hey, are you alright?" a man's voice asked. "Hey, stop that – you're hurting yourself."

I heard, but as if from very far away.

"Come on, now, please stop," he pleaded. Even if I had wanted to stop, by then I couldn't. A crackle of static emitted from his radio. "Yes, this is maintenance. I have a girl here and she's banging her head on the wall in the stairwell. Could you please send Security? She won't respond to me. I can't even tell if she can hear me." He paused, listening. "Yeah, the northeast stairwell in Main."

The man from maintenance stayed with me, at first continuing to try and talk me out of my behaviour. Seeing the futility of it, he stopped and waited for Security to come remedy the problem. Heavy footsteps were soon racing up the stairwell. "Security," one announced. Then they were there, the first one grasping me in a tight embrace from behind, pulling me away.

"No! No! Let me go," I cried out. I struggled, in vain. "No!" The strong men were here. I would not let them win!

Another three guards came up. "Oh, we know her," one said. "Student Health. Come on, we'll bring her to Emergency." And, as always, they win. I'm half-carried, half-dragged down the stairs, along the hallway. People stare – what did this girl do to deserve this treatment? "Watch your step," one says to the other as I stick my foot in front of him to trip him. I was angry.

"Yep, got it."

We rounded the corner to Emergency. They were ready for us; they too knew me well by now. No leaving me in the isolation room. They already had the restraints standing by. Stripped despite my struggles, I again had the flashing thought that the nurses shouldn't be undressing me naked in front of the all-male Security team. But I guess there was no way around that given my intense effort to escape.

"Shush, girl," a quiet and steady voice said to my right. "Quiet, now. Save your strength for later." He repeated himself, over and over. I wanted to react to this kind voice. Everyone else was so harsh, aggressive in the face of my struggling. But I couldn't quite disengage from the situation and be calm. Then two nurses were ready, each with a needle for me.

"One, two," they counted, sticking me twice, together, one on each side.

"NO!" I screamed at the top of my lungs in the moment between the alcohol swabs and the injections. "No, no rats, no rats!" I needed help. "They put rats in me!" I accused. I clawed desperately at my spine as I felt the rats flow up and into my brain.

"Pity, isn't it," a nurse said under her breath to two others. "She's a student – neuropsychiatry. Smart girl. I hate to see her like this. What a shame."

"Really?" another nurse said, and turned to me. "You're taking neuropsychiatry?" I heard her question, heard the whisperings, but could not respond. I was in another world, battling rats.

"Yeah, but at least it's not as bad as last time," one Security guard commented as the Ativan and loxapine, an anti-psychotic, flooded my system and I began to quiet. Later, I would be transferred to the PAU cells for another round.

*   *   *

I'm not sure where the suicidal thoughts came from. I hadn't really thought of ending my life for the last year or two. The thought just wasn't in me and then there it was, as vivid as it had been back in Halifax. "Go on, Erin. Just do it. Come on, we've been waiting," the Voices whispered. Growing louder, they gave me instructions: "In the bathroom. Doorknob. Panties, twisted, noosed. Go, go! Hurry! Before they know." Inside the bathroom, I did as I was told. I stepped out of my panties and put my pyjama bottoms back on. *I'd at least be found decent*, I thought. I put one leg hole over my head and wound the rest tightly. It was just the right length, I discovered happily. The makeshift noose encircled my pale neck and I reached up to slip the other leg hole over the doorknob. Hanging freely, my bottom couldn't quite touch and I sat, suspended, hanging, suffocating.

Suffocating! My vision blurred at the edges, darkness moving towards centre. It was real – I was hanging. "Die, die," a male Voice chanted. "Stupid girl, you're going to die. Die!" But no – that was what They wanted, not me. I wanted to live. *Don't kill me!* I protested.

"You need to die, bitch. Come on, don't hesitate!"

But no, please, let me not die, please.

"You die. Got it? I say you die, you die."

Noooo, I cried. I brought my feet back under me, raising myself out of danger.

"Stupid girl! Don't you dare stop. You do this right! Go die. Go die!" he shrieked at me. I released my feet. I began to hang again. But no – *help me, I don't want to die.*

"You die, you die, you die," a multitude of Voices demanded. I wavered back and forth from obedience to Them and assertion of my right to live. First They'd harass me, convince me, to do Their bidding. Then, I come to my senses and to my intense desire to be true to myself and not be slave to the whims of Them.

It was during a moment of obedience to the Voices that the nurse knocked on the door. "Erin, are you in there?" He waited for a reply. "Erin? Erin? Are you okay?"

I couldn't answer. The Voices were winning.

A key turned in the lock. He had to push the door forcibly to move my body as it hung from the knob. Seeing my limp body, he cried out to someone behind him as he bent quickly to lift me from the strangulation. He grabbed the noose off and my breath came back to me. He propped me up and, with help of another nurse, was ready to help me back to my room. He let go and I crumpled in a heap in the doorway. What was going on? I couldn't focus. But I let myself be helped back to my feet and was prodded towards the cell ward.

"Come on, Erin, I know you can walk fine," one of the nurses snapped irritably. I was stumbling repeatedly on my feet, unsure of what direction to go. Everything was

155

black and I couldn't see.

"I can't see," I answered.

"Open your eyes," she said meanly. Hmm, yeah my eyes had been shut. I opened them. Now I could see. How dumb was I that I couldn't figure out that I couldn't see because I had my eyes shut? Maybe the Voices had a point in calling me stupid.

*   *   *

So it was back to the cells and solitary confinement. Everything had been taken out of my room and then they announced that they were going to check my body for hidden tools of self-harm. *That is,* they said, *please lift your shirt and lower your bottoms.* They checked thoroughly, everywhere. What more shamefulness could they put me through? They were rewarded, though. A razor blade that I had hidden since admission dropped out of my sock when they held it upside-down. This was the only time they strip-searched me. Lucky for me, since other times I did indeed sneak in razor blades, lab-sharp but sterile and wrapped with cardboard, in my vagina.

They went through my bare room. They took my bed apart, took away the blankets. Crouching, I pushed my mattress back to the corner. I held my Bear tightly, my only piece of comfort. "We'll have to check your bear, Erin," the nurse said. He was backed by a small fleet of Security guards.

"No!" I protested. They reached for him. "No! Not my Bear!" I cried as my voice rose hysterically. "No, no!"

"Erin, quit being ridiculous," a nurse said, perturbed. "Now let us see your bear and we'll give him right back. Come on."

"Noooo," I wailed and clung desperately to him. I was having visions of my Bear being torn apart, shedding foam guts and brains. They pried my fingers away and took him hostage. My cries became desperate screams, frantic. Just as they had said, he was quickly examined and given back to me. I huddled with my Bear back into my corner like an animal in fear.

The nurses and Security guards left the room, drawing the door closed behind them lest I leap out and run towards freedom. I remained in my corner. I noticed that all blankets were taken from my bed and I had only a sheet with which to warm myself in the cold cell. Even the pillowcase had been confiscated. Why?

To get the nurses' attention when we are locked up we are supposed to knock quietly on the door. Through a small, break-proof window we watch them, able to see when they hear us. Determined to get at least a blanket to keep me warm – a basic right, I thought – I knocked. And knocked. Louder. I could see my nurse right there at the desk five feet away. Surely he could hear me. *Knock, knock, knock. Why won't you acknowledge me?*

Knocking passed into my slamming my fists against the door and deteriorated to thrashing my leg, my knee, my hands. The door shook loudly. I didn't raise my voice, though. I was silent as I pounded, angry and bruising. No results. I was livid. My head, I thought finally. Smash my head. That will certainly make them move. So I did it.

The nurse didn't notice the change to head-banging right away. Sounds the same. They'd have to see me in the monitor. The first few bashings opened my scab and blood pooled on the door, so much that a thick trickle ran down the light blue concrete and another streaked through my dirty hair.

I got heard, finally. They came in and I said that I wanted blankets; they said that I had to *be good* for them.

"Sit on your bed and be quiet." Soon after, I got my blankets. I made my bed and lay down to sleep.

Now, as I write weeks later, I still have that round, red scar on my forehead. I see it every time I look in the mirror, vaguely fascinated by the indelible memory written on my own flesh. I have many scars from cutting, but those aren't immediately obvious to anyone looking at me. I wonder what people think happened to me. When asked what happened, I state simply that I "banged my head." A beautiful trick of the language: it could be interpreted as passive or active. Would most people assume the former? I wasn't quite sure. Didn't much matter. It was more of a curiosity to me than a concern.

*   *   *

I noticed that I had been put back on the risperidone. I refused it regularly because it had rats in it and They wouldn't let me. (Who are "they" the doctors still wanted to know. The rats? No, stupid, They are not the rats. You would know, if you really listened.) The battle became predictable:

Nurse brings Seroquel and risperidone for my nighttime meds.

I carefully pick the Seroquel pills out of the med cup and take them willingly.

"Take the risperidone, Erin."

"No."

"If you don't take it, you'll get an injection."

"No."

"Come on, now. Stop this silliness." Exasperation.

"No."

Nurse leaves. I fill with denial of the inevitable.

Nurse returns, flanked by Security and needles. Ativan in one. This time, the other was an anti-psychotic that lasts three days: zuclopenthixol. One form of this typical anti-psychotic (read: old – from the '60s) can be used as a long-acting intramuscular anti-psychotic (two to three weeks), and is used primarily in patients with a history of noncompliance; a slightly different chemical form can provide two to three days of sedation. Three days of sedation from one needle? Scary to think what other effects it might have. Perhaps another reason they gave it to me was because it helped "manage" aggression. For a while, I was getting this zuclopenthixol every three days. It really made me understand the term "chemical restraint."

Armed with their needles of sedation, they always won. So why didn't I just take the damn pills myself and avoid the whole scene? Wasn't taking the medication voluntarily easier than being held down and injected, crying and screaming? Yet, irrationally, I always hoped that this time, they'd leave me alone. Besides, the Voices echoed unanimously the perils of taking those pills. Did They fear Their obliteration or did They just enjoy the injection show?

Whatever. I had early on learned to make a big fist while they were applying the restraints, causing the wrist restraints to be a bit loose; as soon as the staff was gone, I narrowed my hands and slid them defiantly out. Then, a quick duck out from under the chest strap, and on to my ankles. I could do it all in less than a minute.

Code White, PAU. Code White, PAU. They'd always discover me free before I could make a run for it. Immediately, they'd call a Code White: aggression. Out came the "hard" restraints, which locked with a key. They at some point realized that the "soft restraints" (made of strong material) were useless on me. I was christened *Houdini* and from then on, I usually had to suffer the chafing hard restraints. These were left tied to a stretcher just outside my room in case of a *problem*.

*   *   *

I was on the PAU ward for about two weeks before I was transferred to UBC. A few more days back on medication left me with simmered-down (though strange: "Let's music the table." Or, "Can we chipmunk black?") Voices and less preoccupation with the rats. My insight was "fleeting" and my judgement was "still of ++ concern." There was still "<u>significant</u>" psychosis but "less evidence of depression."

Soon, it was February. And so, I spent another birthday on a psych ward.

"Happy Birthday, Erin," Richard greeted with a kiss. He came bearing a special meal from the deli, with cheesecake – yum, my favourite – for dessert.

"Thanks, mooncha," I said, using our pet name for each other.

"I just wish you were home," he replied.

"I know. Me too."

"You have presents waiting at home."

"Yeah, I remember that Mom and Dad, and Grammie had sent packages. I'll just have to celebrate when I get out."

"Whenever you want, honey."

"I was thinking," I started, remembering. "Mom and Dad will call to wish me a happy birthday tonight. You can give them the number for here." As before, I had not wanted to tell them about my being in the hospital. I knew that I couldn't ask Richard to lie; I also knew that they would call and call until they got through. So they'd know. I hoped they'd understand and not call too much. It was more than I could *handle*.

They did understand. True, they called later that

evening, but it was not drawn out beyond my limits.

"Hi, Erin," they said together. I could hear the concern, but also a desire to respect my wishes.

"Hi," I answered, cautious.

"Happy birthday." It was strained, knowing that the day was not to be a very Happy one.

"Thanks."

"So...." The pregnant word hung from the phone wires between us, fearing to land anywhere definite.

"So did Richard come in today?"

"Yes. He brought me some special lunch."

"Oh. That sounds good."

"Yup."

"We talked to him earlier. He gave us the number for here."

"Yeah, I told him to."

Silence, heavy.

"So...." Again. So what? I'm on the crazies ward and don't get a proper birthday. So... nothing Happy to say. Bye-bye then.

"It's nice to know he's taking care of you, Erin," Mom began. "I mean, with us so far away, it's reassuring to know he's there for you. He really cares about you, I can tell."

"Yeah." I was not in the mood to talk. A few more awkward sentences and silences later, we hung up.

* * *

I began to get privileges. I had anticipated this all weekend and had my bulimic plans. "We'll start you off with 15 minutes, twice a day, unaccompanied," said Dr. Bradley, my in-hospital psychiatrist for this stay. Could I manage a binge and purge in only fifteen minutes? I was at least going to try. I was pleased to later see in my charts that I was considered "petite... thin." Yet, I still considered myself to be rather large... *fat even.*

My first pass, I walked quickly down to the cafeteria. *Eat, eat, Erin. Faster. Oh look, that woman stares at me cramming it in as fast as I can. Does that guy see me too? Oh they know, but I can't stop to care, no. Just eat, Erin, eat. Did the cashier think anything of my large purchase? Oh the time, hurry, hurry, bulimic bitch. What a sorry sight. Eat, there, last bite, garbage in the can, evidence gone. Go, go – fast, get to your bathroom. How much time? Damn, it's fifteen already and I haven't even purged it yet. Fingers claw the back of my throat. Come on, come up. No, that's not all of it, keep going, Erin. It's so late but I have to finish. So much food inside, have to get it all out. Please, no one come in. There, done, wash my face and hand and dry my eyelashes and put my ring back on my finger and pop a breath mint in, no evidence. Up, back at the ward: clock: time's at 22 minutes. Okay? I'm back, nurse. And she doesn't notice I'm late. So can I do it again?*

Again.

And again.

The bulimic monster lives, fat and feasting.

Chapter 13: Being Rational

Then, I am Decertified and Discharged – a diagonal line slashes through the original certification, signed by Dr. Bradley – and I am home.

At home I had yet much to do on our upcoming wedding. I was getting very frustrated. Richard's sister, Rosa, and his mother, Georgina, were taking over. It was to be a repeat of last summer, when Rosa got married, it seemed: same hall, same food, same wine making, same array of (to me) unknown people. My guest list was between 30 and 40 people; Richard's was over 100 and growing since Georgina kept inviting people without telling me.

There were many details Rosa "helped" me with. I didn't want to carry flowers – she called a florist and set up an appointment. I was fine with no flower girls – Rosa asked three, plus a ring bearer (whom I never met). She scoffed at my shoes (too plain), my dress (too white), and even my eyebrows (needed plucking). She called several times a day. Nevertheless, I was getting excited.

* * *

As I had hoped, I defended for my Master's degree in

May of 2005. I thought it went well, until my committee members began questioning my methods. According to them, I had used imprecise and out-dated ways of counting cells. But I had been taught in the lab that that was how to do it. I wondered what Andrew was thinking. Was he mentally taking responsibility? He didn't say anything, not even when the committee decided that they would accept my thesis only if I took the cell count data completely out. All I'd have left, then, were the behavioural studies. Still, they passed me. I could now add those letters, MSc, to my name. I felt proud. I had done it! Despite Voices and hospitals, Trackers and medications, I was going to receive, in November's convocation, my second university degree.

*   *   *

As I began to think about my future PhD work on schizophrenia, my mind wandered over to a long-buried thought. I recalled that one journal, *Schizophrenia Bulletin*, had a section for patients to write about their own experiences with the disease. *First Person Accounts* documented such stories to aid professionals in their quest to truly understand what it is like living with the diseases they study and treat. I had read several *Accounts* as an undergrad at MSVU for my fourth-year term paper on childhood-onset schizophrenia that later won that year's Library Award for best undergraduate paper. The stories brought a sense of reality to the paper and its corresponding lecture I gave for my Childhood Psychopathology seminar. Now, I thought, it could be my turn to share.

The next day, I checked the journal's homepage. The guidelines for author section noted that for *Accounts* the paper had to have a point; submissions could not be vague, unfocused, or rambling.

164

I let this guideline simmer amongst my memories. I had many experiences that could be written up as stories, but that was not directed enough. I had to pull some theme or lesson from these varied experiences. Slowly, one emerged, percolating. I began to write.

"Hey, Daniel," I greeted as he came into the lab. He had come for an after-hours writing session and I was putting the finishing touches on my manuscript. "I'm working on a paper, a different one."

"What's it for?" he asked.

"Have you heard of the journal *Schizophrenia Bulletin*?"

"Yeah, I have."

"Well, they have this *First Person Accounts* section that's written by patients with schizophrenia. You know, to help professionals understand what living with schizophrenia is really like."

"Sounds like a good idea. So you're writing one?"

"Yes, just finishing it up now. Could you read it for me a bit later? It's short – only two pages." I added in case he was swamped with work.

"Sure, I'd love to."

"Great. I'll give it to you in... maybe ten or so minutes."

"Okay." He settled down at another computer and we lapsed into silence. I finished the paper and edited it through until I was happy with it. Soon the printer was transcribing my manuscript into paper-and-ink.

"Here it is," I said.

"Thanks." As he read, my fears haggled me. Was it good enough, captivating, and interesting? Did I make my point clearly? Moreover, was it a point worth making? I watched, unsettled, as he read my words:

Being Rational

By Erin Kopialo

I was awash in a sea of irrationality. The Voices swirled around me, teaching me their Wisdom. Their Wisdom was of the Deep Meaning and I struggled to understand. They told me their secrets and insights, piece by piece. Slowly, I was beginning to make sense of it all. It was no delusion, I knew - in contrast to what the doctors said.

"Erin, you are a scientist," they'd begin. "You are intelligent, rational. Tell me, then, how can you believe that there are rats inside your brain? They're just plain too big. Besides, how could they get in?"

They were right. About my being intelligent, I mean; I was, after all, a graduate student in the Neuroscience program at the University of British Columbia. But how could they relate that rationality to the logic of the Deep Meaning? For it was due to the Deep Meaning that the rats had infiltrated my system and were inhabiting my brain. They gnawed relentlessly on my neurons, causing massive degeneration. This was particularly upsetting to me, as I depended on a sharp mind for my work in Neuroscience.

They spent significant periods of time consuming brain matter in the occipital lobe of my brain. I knew, from my studies, that this was the primary visual cortex. And yet, I experienced no visual deficits. Obviously, I realized, I had a very unique brain: I was able to regenerate large sections of my central nervous system – and to do so extremely quickly. I relaxed a bit, but not entirely. Surely no good could come of having rats feed on my brain cells. So I sought means of ridding my body of them. I bled them out through self-cutting and banging my head until the skin broke, bloody. Continually, I kept my brain active, electrocuting the rats that happened to be feasting on the activated neurons.

"As a neuroscientist, how can you believe all this?" the doctors queried.

"Because it is all of the Deep Meaning."

"But it doesn't make sense. It's irrational. You surely know that."

"Because," I replied deliberately, as if talking to a child. "The Deep Meaning transcends scientific logic." How else could it be true? I did know all the logical limitations of my ideas, but I was also receiving such intense messages that the rats and my regenerating brain were also true. So I rationally concluded that the one supersedes the other. Still, I could use some of my scientific understanding to deal with that which the Deep Meaning imposed on me. Like the electrocution: I knew that when neurons are activated, they transmit signals using electrical current. I therefore reasoned that, since the rats were so small, on the order of magnitude of a neuron, they would experience the electricity as violent and perhaps fatal.

My understanding of my regenerating brain was similarly based on biological knowledge. If function, such as sight, is not impaired despite significant cell loss, there are two possible explanations: remaining cells may compensate for the damage, or there is rapid regeneration. My logical mind gave me these possibilities and then the Deep Meaning proceeded to inform me which was true. I thus learned that I was part of a Great Experiment. Since no other case of such capacities for regeneration in the brain are known in the scientific community, there would be considerable interest in studying mine. Scientifically, I knew that the proper examination of my abilities was of immense value, and therefore did not object to the more bothersome aspects of the Great Experiment – like a diet restricted

167

to foods with Deep Meaning such as carrots (a car rots the environment), cereal (to "c" (see) what is real), or cookies that, at different coffee shops, are alternatively known as "Morning Madness" or "Morning Glory" (what some – i.e. doctors - called my madness was actually my glory).

The rats weren't the only thing that bothered me. My neighbour across the alley spied continually on me. He wanted to kill me, I learned from the Voices and the Deep Meaning. Scared, I put up some dark curtains. I slept well that night but awoke to a terrifying truth: the night before, he had entered my room and installed a tracking devise into my abdomen. Now he could track me everywhere; there was no more hiding.

The doctors latched onto this story, eager to show me the irrationality of it all. How could he have gotten in? My door and windows had been locked and there was no sign of tampering. I answered from the Deep Meaning that had revealed it to me.

"He atomized himself."

"Atomized?"

"Yes. You know – when you dismantle something into its component atoms, pass these tiny pieces through the barrier, and reassemble them again on the other side." Didn't physics have some similar concepts?

"And the tracker in your abdomen?"

"Atomization again. Otherwise there'd be an incision," I reasoned, rational. But the doctors concluded differently. Delusion and paranoia were their words, their explanations.

And there are many other such stories. Each time, I would be able to evaluate things from two perspectives: my scientific logic and the explanation from the Deep Meaning. As the doctors would say, these corresponded to rationality and irrationality, respectively. But, given the input I had from Voices (auditory hallucinations, the doctors say) and the immense feelings of truth from the Deep Meaning, I was in fact fighting to preserve my *rationality in the face of the irrational. I valued my logical mind so dearly that when it began to be challenged by schizophrenic hallucinations, delusions, and disorders of the ability to ascribe meaningfulness, I used everything available to me to try and figure out what were the most rational explanations. I craved rationality, and rationality to me was taking all evidence and making conclusions. Even if they didn't conform to everyone else's ideas of what is rational, I was fighting to maintain, at the very least, the integrity of my own rationality.*

Anti-psychotic medication has helped to distance me from the Voices and the Deep Meaning. While I never quite give up these as irrational, I am aware that they influence my ideas of, and my actions in response to, rationality. I have come to believe that in order to truly understand others, be they schizophrenic or otherwise, we must not only discover their thoughts, feelings, and actions but we must look to understand how they connect these into a coherent structure, and to recognize that no matter what this structure looks like, it is the product of a rational mind.

"This is great, Erin," he declared when he looked up, finished, from the pages. "It's quite descriptive and it's a good read; I hope they accept it."

"Thanks," I said, accepting his praise, then, insecure, I asked, "Is the point clear?"

"Oh, completely. I liked it. It's true: we all try to make rational sense out of our experiences, even if they are schizophrenic episodes."

"Exactly." I felt good. Daniel and I talked a bit longer, after which I packed up my bags to go home. It was getting late; I could submit the paper tomorrow.

"Bye, Daniel," I said as I opened the door.

"Bye."

As I walked home slowly, savouring the rich feeling

of having accomplished something worthwhile, I wondered about what name I should use on the paper. By the time it would be printed, I'd be married and I planned on taking Richard's last name, Kopialo. It just felt right to submit it under that name.

The next day, I stayed late to submit the paper. It was simple and fast and, again, I left satisfied. Now just to wait.

Chapter 14: No More MHT, No More Abuse

I reached for my medications sleepily. It was past midnight and I was tired. The Seroquel was where it was supposed to be on the bedside table, but not the loxapine I was also now taking. *Oh, well, I'll find it tomorrow,* I promised myself and rolled over and quickly fell asleep.

By the next morning, I had forgotten the missing loxapine, and didn't remember that I needed to search for it until nighttime, when I was again tired and in no mood to rifle through things looking for a little bottle of green pills.

This repeated itself for several nights, but I thought little of it. Instead, I began noticing little things, like a rustling of rats in the back of me head and the whispers of Voices. They began making senseless, random comments to me throughout the day and especially as I tried to go to sleep or wake up. "Did you rabbit the squirrel?" They asked, or, "Watch the table, it will grow up tall." At least they weren't attacking me with derogatory comments or threatening me.

I didn't quite know how to react. They were infrequent enough and calm enough that I didn't have to pay them much attention. Still, this combined with

increasing difficulties remembering things and following a conversation worried me. I had to start protecting my brain again. I produced the needed radio static to foil anyone who wanted to access my thoughts and memories and felt relatively safe.

I should have told Richard. I was scared, though. He had said that he couldn't handle me being sick again. *It wasn't as if it was getting serious*, I reasoned. *I'd tell him if it was, right?* I asked myself, trying to justify my silence. He didn't detect my anxiety.

A few days later, I spied a small pill bottle among Richard's mess. Oh – the loxapine I had been looking for. I had completely forgotten about it over the last couple of days. I'd better start taking them again, I thought. I did resume it that night, but it wasn't until a few days later that I realized that my recent experiences may have been linked to the lack of loxapine for a week. This insight came as I noticed that things such as the waking rats, annoying Voices, and problems of cognition began to ameliorate. A little while later, I realized the connection between my little green pills and symptoms.

It reminded me of my first experience with anti-psychotic drugs. Back at the NS, I was told they were going to begin treatment with the anti-psychotic risperidone. I had had no idea what that meant. I had not known what it would change. But I soon noticed that life was easier. As with the loxapine incident years later, and several times of similar drug use/symptom severity correlations, I could recognize that yes, the medications were effective and beneficial.

Maybe this time I would remember this little fact, I

thought. It scared me to think that I could, by neglect, land myself in the hospital again. I vowed to take the medications, no matter what. I just couldn't risk the hospital. How would Richard cope? How could I stand it? Much better to take the pills. I simply could not risk losing my sanity and my relationship with Richard.

*   *   *

My current psychiatrist, Dr. Musly, would no longer see me; she was "unable to continue follow-up." *I must have been a difficult patient*, I concluded. I was called "unpredictable" by the doctors in the hospital, whatever that meant. So I was sent to my first Mental Health Team (MHT).

I don't remember much about my case manager, but the obnoxious, arrogant psychiatrist, Dr. Lowes, lives vividly in my memory. I spent the first few sessions in my usual silence. This really irritated him and he began insulting me. "You're too smart to have schizophrenia," he scoffed. I said nothing. "You don't have to take your meds, if you don't want to. It's your choice, Erin."

A choice? Yes, in a sense it was: I was the one putting the little pills in my mouth and swallowing them with a gulp of water. I was the one who was often non-compliant with my meds. However, I was learning, albeit slowly and with much resistance, that the medicines were keeping my schizophrenia at bay. Psychiatrists, nurses, family, and even friends urged me to take my medications regularly, faithfully. Dr. Lowes did not.

The implication was that my choice was thus: take pills, be well versus don't take pills, be well. However, no matter what Dr. Lowes suggested, I knew that that was not a choice I had. I had schizophrenia and like it or not I needed to be on relatively high doses of anti-psychotics to remain well. History had repeated itself over and over: my choice was to take my meds, and be well or not take them and end up psychotic, delusional, and restrained in a hospital with a bloody forehead and injections in my butt. *Choice?*

I continued not to talk while he jeered at me for my "fake" schizophrenia and my waste of his time. There was no psychotherapy, no compassion, no hope.

One Tuesday I had an appointment with both Tayar, my case manager at the MHT, and Dr. Lowes. I was not looking forward to this at all. I cowered in the waiting room, dreading the inevitable. "Erin, you can come in now," Tayar called and I rose obediently but resentfully.

"Hello, Erin," Dr. Lowes greeted as I settled in a chair in his office. Through his window I could see blue skies with a touch of greyish clouds. *Oh, to be a bird and fly away from it all, to be a Care Bear living up in the cloud land of Care-A-Lot,* I thought as I gazed out and up.

"Erin?"

"Umhmm." We set off on the usual path of questions. I would only answer with a nod or shake of my head. It was hard to follow what Dr. Lowes and Tayar were saying. And really, I wasn't sure I wanted to follow. I just wanted out.

"About medication, then," Dr. Lowes said a few torturous minutes later. "Are you happy with what you're on?"

I gave him a puzzled glance, avoiding his eyes. I didn't want to risk a mind-reading or worse.

"Your medications. Do you want to continue on the 1400 mg a day of the Seroquel and the – " he consulted my chart – "loxapine at 10 mg a day?"

"In the past, every time I've gone off or reduced my

medications, I've ended up in the hospital. And I'm *not* going to the hospital again." How could they want me to end up there again?

"No, of course not. We don't want you in the hospital," Dr. Lowes said. I was suspicious. "However, it's your choice."

"Well?" he asked.

"Keep... same..." my voice trailed off into oblivion.

"You want to keep with the Seroquel?"

I nodded.

"And the loxapine? It's only 10 mg a day." Was he implying that since it was a lower dose it was unnecessary? I thought back a few weeks, when I had lost my loxapine and had therefore gone without for many days. I had worsened then, I had realized in retrospect. To me that said that it was necessary.

"I did not take it for a little while. Last month," I began. "That... That was the time... I couldn't... it was bad...." I couldn't get a coherent sentence out. "And... it wasn't that I went off it and then said to myself, I'm off medication so I should be sick," I added. "It was, I'm not doing as well, and then realizing that I hadn't been taking it." There. That was enough talking. I lapsed into another silence.

"Okay, then. Seroquel, loxapine. I'll phone in a month's supply with three repeats. Good?"

I nodded. He dialled, waited, and left the order with the pharmacist. Appointment over. As much as I resented how they often trivialized my illness and my supposed control over its symptoms, I had to appreciate that he let me decide what and how much medication he'd phone in to the pharmacy.

* * *

175

I checked the author log for *Schizophrenia Bulletin* in late August. Surely they'd have a decision by now, I thought. I scanned the summary of manuscript status.

"Strange," I said aloud. There was no record of my submission at all. What was going on? My first inclination was conspiracy theory: someone didn't want my paper published. They were plotting against me and would soon come to punish me, or send someone after me. "No, Erin," I admonished myself aloud. "Think logically... *rationally*." Okay. What would be the right response? *Ask them,* I heard in my mind. Right: I could email and ask if they had received it. I set to it.

I got my answer the next morning when I checked my email:

"Dear Erin Hawkes, We have no record of your manuscript. Perhaps it did not upload properly, or some such problem. Please resubmit."

So I resubmitted. Two days later, I received another email. A smile spread over my face and I cheered instantly. Accepted! Moreover, it was accepted *"as is;"* I had no revisions to make. Accepted, accepted, accepted!

"Accepted!" I said happily when I got home. "They accepted my schizophrenia paper!" Richard grinned.

"That's awesome, Erin!"

"Yes. No revisions, either. They liked it as is."

"Good for you. When will they publish it?"

"I'm not sure. A few months is my guess."

"Well, let's celebrate." He disappeared into the kitchen and emerged with a bottle of red wine and two glasses. "To Erin!"

"And to her mooncha!" We drank to that. Later, I went though the same conversation with Daniel, and then

Melissa. My support system, happy for me. It felt good.

*   *   *

I couldn't hear them, but I felt a rustling. Were they waking up? No, please no. I couldn't handle another assault from the rats. They had been sleeping so peacefully there in the back of my head. *Please stay sleeping*, I wished.

*   *   *

It was another dreaded trip to the MHT. Here I was again, waiting for Tayar. At least the check-in was just with her; Dr. Lowes met with me less frequently.

"Come on in, Erin," she said a minute or two later. I followed her, mute, sat down, crossed my legs, and found a safe spot for my eyes to focus on. "So," she said suggestively. "How are you?"

"Medium."

"Uh hum. Can you elaborate? What has happened since we last met?"

So I was supposed to say something now. "I started in my new lab, on my PhD." There, that was something for her. But she wanted more. I was supposed to be working on my *issues*. What these were, I wasn't quite sure. I was willing to work on them, but I needed help identifying them and this was not being provided.

As I sat there, stressed, the Voices began to speak up. "Shhh, Erin. Don't say too much. Lest is best, lest is best." I listened to Them, worried. What might They do if I dared disobey? I looked up at Tayar. She was chatting, pseudo-nice. I heard her voice rise at the end of her speech. A question.

How to answer? I mustn't talk more than I absolutely had to, I knew. On top of it all, she was looking at me. If I raised my eyes, they'd meet hers... and the mind-reading would begin, the foraging through my thoughts, the

177

destruction. I couldn't risk that. I kept my gaze downward.

"Erin? Are you going to answer my question?" she pushed. *No*, I replied wordlessly. "Shut up, shut up, you little slut," the Voices rhymed off in the background. "Don't give her anything to use against you. And don't look up – she's poised ready to mind-read, mind-fuck, you're out of luck." I hated it when they waxed poetic.

I sat, unspeaking, unmoving. Soon, Tayar's stream of speech ended as well. She sat back, waiting. *Oh, I see*, I thought to myself. *She's using that psychoanalytic tactic of "I'll-be-quiet-until-it-drives-the-patient-to-talk."* Too bad that one didn't work on me. I could out-silence anyone, particularly when I was being threatened by the Voices not to talk.

Five minutes, ten; did we make it to fifteen? Then, taking a pen and paper, she wrote something down. She held the scrap of paper up to me. I read it:

"Are you going to talk any more?"

I shook my head. She sighed, turned to her desk. "Why not?"

"I'm not allowed," I answered carefully.

"Oh?"

I said nothing. She waited. I listened to the Voices again. They were men's Voices this time, one coming from my right and one from my left. Sometimes they spoke in unison, sometimes individually. "Don't tell her. She's the Enemy. Shhh, shhh. No words allowed, stupid girl."

Eventually, we made it out to the reception area. "When do you want to come back?"

Never, I answered in my head.

"Three weeks or four?"

Four, of course four. "Four."

"Okay, how about October 11th? 3:00? I nodded and

accepted the reminder slip. I left quickly, quietly. Free again! I went and bought a small package of chocolate chip cookies to help drown my upset in processed sugar.

"How was your day?" Richard asked when he arrived home.

"Fine, except for my appointment," I replied negatively.

"What happened?"

"Oh, just the usual. You know, they tell me I need to work on my *issues* but then won't help me figure out what they are," I answered. "They don't *hear* me. So I stopped talking."

"You should get another psychiatrist," Richard suggested.

"As if I haven't been though enough of them," I said almost in tears.

"Come here, honey," he said supportively, and drew me close for a hug. What a sweetie I had for a husband.

But this would not last.

*   *   *

I needed a new ID badge so I brought the form over to Photo ID a few buildings over from where my lab was.

"Would you like a new picture, or should I just use the old one?" the woman at the computer asked.

"My old one," I replied. It had been taken when I had been relatively thin; a new one would show my chubby, swollen face. Yuck. A thin Erin's head was printed and I attached it to my key ring I carried around my neck.

"That's a nice lanyard," she said, reaching for it.

"Thanks. I got it at a conference," I replied. She tested its strength.

"Oh, it's not one of the easy-release ones," she noted. "You'd better be careful around the patients."

179

"I don't work with patients," I told her. "And I don't think the mice will grab it," I added cheerfully.

"Well, just stay clear of the psych ward. Those dangerous crazies jump the bushes and run off all the time."

I felt anger welling up inside me. How dare she put down what had caused me so much pain, insult me for being one of those *crazies*. "Yeah, well," I answered noncommittally and left her office. I fumed all the way back to the lab. How could people be so insensitive?

*   *   *

Later that day, I reluctantly opened the door to the MHT waiting room. There were two men there; one was smiling goofily at the wall, and the other was talking loudly to himself. I sat down. I had no hopes for a good appointment; I was already shutting down. By the time Tayar fetched me, I knew I would not be telling her much at all.

She started into the usual questions. It was worse then pulling the proverbial teeth. The Voices were quiet, but I knew from past experiences that They preferred me to be silent too.

"Are you taking your medications?" she probed.

"It doesn't matter," I said. "They're not real."

"What? Not real?"

"Placebos."

"Placebos?" she parroted. It took her a minute to find her next question. "Why do you think that?"

"Because he phones the prescriptions in," I reasoned. I knew that he didn't trust me with a written one, since I'd read it and know. So he must have either pretended to order it when I was in the office (he'd just talk to the dial tone) or if the call was real, he'd phone back right after I left

180

and get them to put placebos in my order. They looked the same as the real ones, of course, so I wouldn't catch on, I knew.

"But then why do you keep coming back?" she asked.

"You keep making me appointments," I told her. "And I don't want to have to pay."

"Pay?" she laughed. "You don't have to pay."

"At my other psychiatrist's, if you missed an appointment, you had to pay."

"Not here."

"Oh."

"So, then, do you want to stop coming?"

Was she dull? What had I been telling them for the past few months? I nodded my head.

"Okay, we can close your file for you." She paused, waiting for a reaction. None forthcoming, she continued. "But if you ever want to come back, just call and make an appointment with the intake worker; she'll re-open your file and we'll take it from there."

I waited for her to finish. She too waited, perhaps hoping that I would crack under the pressure of leaving – sob, sob – this place. Not likely.

"Well, if you don't have anything else to say, you can leave," she said somewhat rudely. So I gathered my bag, stood, and let myself out of her office. I'm not sure if she had really meant what she had said, but I wasn't about to wait around to find out. I walked quickly down the corridor, scared that she would appear and call me back and say that I couldn't just leave, that she'd put me in the hospital for failing her test, or something else absurd. I slipped out the door, took the elevator down, and breathed a sigh of relief. I was never going to deal with Tayar and Dr.

Lowes again. Of that, I was sure.

She phoned later the next week and left a message that she had talked with Dr. Lowes and they were indeed going to close my file. Again, she noted that I could reactivate it whenever I wanted. As if.

*　　*　　*

Richard and I got married that July. I remember the day as a blissful blur: gazing into his honey eyes as we said our vows, stealing kisses. Little did I know then that only a few days later, the abuse would begin. Apparently, just before our honeymoon at my parent's secluded cabin on the cliffs of the Atlantic Ocean, Richard told my Dad that he might have to "divorce your daughter."

Talk of divorce began in earnest when we got back to Vancouver. He would get mad at me, often for no observable reason, and tell me that he wanted a divorce. I'd talk him down, until he was crying and I'm-sorry-ing and clinging to me for dear life.

He began to use crack again, and no longer talked of getting a job (he had been on government disability since we met). He preferred his life of lounging, video-gaming, smoking pot in addition to the crack, and masturbating. I worked hard at the lab on my graduate degree, which I enjoyed. He thought I should go on Disability, too, so we could do his lifestyle together. No, thanks. I had goals. He had promised his own goals before our marriage but refused to follow them once he "had" me.

The abuse was escalating. He had a rich vocabulary of words I would never even think of, but which he used liberally to put down his "sorry excuse for a mate." Although it hurt, I could handle the words, and kept, by my own honour, from hurling any back. He threatened to go get a prostitute to satisfy his perverse sexual fantasies that I refused to humour (although he would force it on me anyway). Sexually ignorant and naïve, I chalked it all up to normal male behaviour. Later, a psychologist would use the word *rape* to describe it.

What scared me, though, was the mounting physical abuse. He pushed me down a few times, threatened to throw me out the window. He'd make moves to punch me in the face, stopping his fist an inch away from my face, citing that he wasn't going to do it because he didn't want evidence. He brought a knife to keep under his pillow at night, knowing that I knew that he had threatened his own sister with a knife before I had even met him. But after the day he put his strong hands around my neck, I got really scared. *I might have to leave,* I thought. I went so far as to leave an overnight bag at Melissa's.

I'm so sorry. I'll never do it again.

There was always another again.

However, as from the beginning of our marriage, I always made the peace, the forgiveness. I promised never to leave him and to never give up on him or our relationship. But by November of 2005, just four months after our wedding, I sat with him and told him plainly that I simply couldn't handle any more abuse – of any kind. He was almost out of chances.

Then, one morning, Richard woke me around 5:30. He didn't like me sleeping; he wanted me to be at his disposal at all times. Annoyed and sleepy, I resisted being wakened. He was ranting about something or other and I tuned him out. "It's too early, Richard," I said. "If you really need to talk about this, we can do it later today, okay?" I turned onto my side, ready to get some more sleep.

Angered, Richard struck out with his usual hurtful

words. "Cunt! Stupid bitch! Fucking psycho!" Numb, I ignored him as one ignores a toddler in a tantrum. He escalated his attack. He turned me towards him forcibly and, bringing his face within inches of my own, he spat.

The insult of that action did not register at first. I instead simply felt the physical sensation of wetness on my face. I wiped it with my hand in disbelief. He had spat in my face?

Before I could process this attack, I felt another wetness on my skin. Richard was standing over me as I lay in bed and was emptying the contents of a bottle of water over me. The absurd childishness of his actions shocked me. "Richard!" I exclaimed, aghast and disgusted. I was certainly awake now and got out of bed. I headed towards the washroom.

"Yeah? Look at this!" Richard yelled. I looked over at him, seething with anger and hurt. *He had spat in my face.*

Still aggressive, he grabbed one of my library books and ripped it repeatedly. Next, he came out of the bedroom holding one of my Care Bears. The big one, Champ Bear – Richard's favourite. He grasped the Bear's neck with his strong hands and started to pull. He looked me straight in the eye with loathing.

"Richard! No!" I cried, reaching for my Bear. Richard pulled him out of my reach. "Richard!" I was yelling now, desperate. It was not so much panic from the impending destruction of the Bear – I could always sew him up, or buy another. It was the fact that Richard knew how much I cherished my Bears, and that he was therefore using them to hurt me.

I got hold of the Bear's leg and pulled him towards me. "Yeah, pull!" Richard sneered. Only the strength of the stitching was preventing the Bear from being torn apart.

We had overnight guests then – a couple whose daughter was in VGH – and the yelling woke them. They came towards us, ready to intervene. Richard saw them and let go. I hugged Champ Bear to me.

I don't exactly remember how it happened, but my next memory is of Richard, subdued and apologetic, trying to convince me that he "really didn't mean it" and was "so sorry." He would "never do it again" and wanted a hug. He spoke softly, sweetly. But I knew this routine. It meant nothing anymore. It could not allay my fears, nor could it kindle any trust within me. Not anymore. Something broke inside me and I knew that there were no more chances for my abusive husband.

My mind was racing. It was time for me to leave, and quickly. I feared his destructive nature and therefore wanted to bring my irreplaceable treasured things with me. *Richard had packed his bag and would probably be leaving too for his usual early morning swim,* I realized. That would give me some time. So I let him hug me and think that all was well. *Just go,* I willed.

He left.

I sprang into action. A part of me had mentally rehearsed what I was about to do. I swiftly opened our new suitcases, emptying them of the Christmas lights they stored. *The lights from our wedding.* I cast them unceremoniously aside. Suitcases ready, I began packing hurriedly. I had about an hour and a half and wanted to be out well before then.

Care Bears, photos, letters, and other keepsakes went into the suitcases. Jodi, the wife staying with us, handed me Care Bear things as she spotted them around the apartment. My heart was racing, terrified that Richard would for some reason return early… what would he do? Surely he would be angry, and that scared me. *Hurry, Erin, hurry.* I got dressed.

Jodi's husband, Tony, helped me bring my four suitcases to their van. I phoned Melissa. It was just before 6:30 am when we pulled up in front of her apartment. Thanking Tony and Jodi, I fled into the safety of Melissa's home.

I had done it.

I had left my abusive husband.

And I knew that I was not going back.

*   *   *

"Hi, Heidi," I said into the phone to my closest friend. I was quiet, sad. I paused, then confessed. "I left Richard this morning."

"Oh, Erin." Heidi's voice was full of compassion.

"Yeah."

"Are you okay?"

"I'm at Melissa's," I said. "But can I come over to your place? Melissa's going to be out all day and I just can't handle being alone right now."

"Sure, of course." Heidi was on maternity leave, staying home with her young daughter. Being with both of them would be most reassuring.

"I'll leave as soon as I get my stuff together." I hesitated, tears welling up. "We'll talk when I get there."

"Okay. See you soon."

"Bye."

"Bye. Take care."

I hung up. Soon, I was on the bus. My head and heart were full to bursting with emotion and a few stubborn tears worked their way down my cheeks. *I had left Richard.* My world would never be the same again. Was that a good thing? I missed him terribly already – but feared him more.

Another part of my mind was preoccupied about what Richard's reaction would be when he returned from swimming. It would certainly be obvious what I had done, and Tony and Jodi would confirm it. Would he be angry? Sad? Hurt? I didn't know, and I didn't care. From now on, he would be in the past.

*　*　*

I wanted to get the rest of my belongings. Melissa, Daniel (who had a car), and Juan from the lab were ready to help. Two days later, I picked a time Richard was least likely to be home and we went in. It was eerie, returning, as it were, to the scene of the crime. I had judged correctly: Richard was not there.

We loaded Daniel's car several times and made trips to the storage unit I had rented to house my things until I found a new place to live. Soon, we were gathering up the last few bags and boxes when I heard a key in the lock. Richard! Careless so near the end, we had left the deadbolt undone. "Lock it!" I cried to Juan, who was standing closest to the door. He lunged and pulled it across just in time. Richard opened the door, but only the few inches allowed by the bolt.

"Erin?"

"Yes?" I answered shakily. I was beside the door, heart pounding. "I'm getting my stuff," I said. "We're almost done."

"Let me in," he demanded.

"I'd really rather not," I replied.

"Erin...."

"Please, Richard. Please just go and let us finish."

Richard's voice softened. "Erin, I'm not going to hurt you. Trust me." Tears streamed down my face. "I love you, Erin. I just want to talk to you. I'm sorry, really. Just please let me see you."

I hesitated, and unlocked the door. Richard entered. He took me into his arms and pressed me close. My body melted into his, into that familiar comfort and warmth. *My husband.* How I loved him and wanted things to just be okay again.

He took my hand and led me into the bedroom. "Erin, please come back," he pleaded quietly. "I miss you so much. I'm going crazy without you. I need you, Erin. I'm sorry. Please forgive me, please, Erin." His tears caught in his throat and his voice wavered. "Erin…."

I was crying; full, deep sobs racked my body until it trembled. "No, Richard. I'm afraid of you. I can't trust you." I looked up at him. Gently, he caught a tear as it trickled down my face and wiped it away.

"I need you, Erin. I can't live without you." His own tears flowed freely now, his beautiful long lashes glistening, wet. My heart cried out and I touched his cheek lovingly. *My mooncha.* But as much as I felt my love for him, and his for me, I knew that his tears and gentle words were not enough. I pulled away, stood up. I walked slowly to the living room where Daniel and Melissa stood. My heart was being wrenched apart and I could not stop crying.

Then things changed. Richard came out and, delusional, assumed that Daniel and Melissa were in on some conspiracy against him. His anger rose, defiant. He remembered Melissa and her mother's refusal to help him get in touch with me over the weekend. "I'm really not impressed with Melissa," he told me well within earshot of her. "And her mother." He turned and said something to Melissa as he left the apartment.

"That's rich," she said, angry and disgusted with him. He had some nasty reply, which got a rise out of her, while he walked down the hall.

I will always remember what Melissa said next. It rang clear, loud, and full of emotion along the corridor. "Fuck you, Richard!" she hurled at him. Never having been able to do it myself, I felt a sense of satisfaction through her contempt. I looked at Melissa.

"Thanks."

Shaken and afraid of Richard returning in anger, we each grabbed a final load and fled to the car. *Hurry, hurry!* I thought, panicky.

All three of us couldn't fit in the front seats of Daniel's car. "Sit on my lap," I told Melissa but it didn't work. So we "walked" her partway home, following her closely in the car as she walked at her usual brisk pace.

Daniel and I headed back to the storage locker. We were both crying now. Seeing Richard had aroused such a mixture of emotions and they overwhelmed me. My shoulders shook as I sobbed and Daniel lay a comforting hand on my knee.

*   *   *

Daniel and Melissa treated me to dinner at a nice restaurant on Forrest Street. The food was good, but I had little appetite. We exchanged small talk and it refreshed my broken spirit but the coming evening hung over me. While Richard and I had talked, I had asked for my things back that he had taken out of spite the day between my leaving and when I came back to the apartment for the rest of my things: things that were clearly mine, and not ours. We had arranged to meet at his mother's house at 8:00 that night. Daniel drove and stayed close by as a difficult series of exchanges took place.

Rosa and her husband, Drew, were there, self-proclaimed mediators. "Now," Rosa began, launching into

189

a short speech. "We're here to help you communicate and listen to each other. None of us want you to split up. Remember, marriage is about compromise. We want you each to have a turn to say what's on your mind and then to listen to the other. It's not about Erin getting her way or Richard getting his. You both have to meet halfway. Okay?" She looked at each of us in turn.

"Fine," Richard said, anger in his voice.

"Richard, what do you want to say to Erin?" But he was up and headed out the door.

"I'm going for a smoke," he said curtly.

Rosa was annoyed but it gave me a chance to explain to them why had I left. They had heard some of the things Richard had done to me – he had boasted about spitting at me, just as he had about pulling a knife on Rosa. But they did not know about the extent of the emotional abuse: the names, the threats, as well as the physical abuse. I didn't tell about the sexual abuse, feeling at once embarrassed and also still believing that it was normal. Even Rosa was quiet as I told what had been going on.

By the time Richard had come back in, they were more on my side than their initial sitting on the fence. They realized that it was no longer about compromise but about safety. They descended on Richard.

"What you are doing to her is not right," Rosa started. "There's no excuse for it. None."

Richard became defensive. "She emotionally abused me, too. She's so cold. I was just trying to get her to respond to me."

By this point, I was sobbing again. Georgina fussed with some tea in front of me but I couldn't even hold a cup steadily. "Look what you're doing to her," Drew said in my defence. "Look at her."

"What do you want to say?" Rosa asked me.

I took a deep breath. "I want my things," I began, shaky but determined. "Richard took some things that are clearly mine, and only mine. I want them back, please." I addressed the last sentence to Richard.

"What things?"

"My quilt. My degree. That wicker basket and the papers in it. DVDs. And one of the wedding albums. There were two," I explained to our referees. "One from the photographer and one I made of the New Brunswick reception. I was thinking that you could keep the photographer's and I would keep the other one. It's only fair."

"Do you have these things of hers?" Rosa asked Richard.

By this point, he was crouched at my knee. He spoke soothingly. "Of course I'll give you your things, mooncha," he said. "I'm not trying to take them from you." True to his word, he left and returned with my quilt. I hugged it close, its familiarity and rescue from near-loss comforting me.

Daniel drove me and my recovered things back to Melissa's for the night. I am forever grateful for their compassion and help.

*   *   *

The rats were back. I felt them scurrying about in my head, hungry. My vulnerable neurons cowered.

No, please, not the rats.

"Yes," said a Voice.

The Voices - They were back too?

"Yes, girl, stupid girl," They chanted. "Little fuck-up, sit up."

I was on the bus, headed nowhere. I had missed my stop for work, unable to move myself from my seat. No will, no care. Now I knew why. The Voices were back. I had been taking medication, but somewhat sporadically as I usually do when under stress. Moreover, I think that stress itself lessens the efficacy of the drugs.

"Girl, stupid girl. We send the rats, you know."

The bus reached the end of its run and I got off mechanically. Onto another. Ride, slide, abide. Was it Their rhyme or mine? The wheels on the bus go round. I go round. Found?

I arrived late at Daniel's, where I was now staying, not wanting to over-stay at any one friend's house. I said little, exhausted from the Voices. I picked up my book and read. Did I want to talk, Daniel wanted to know. *No, thanks. Too overwhelming.*

He and his roommate, Luke, soon left together to go to a friend's house. I tried to concentrate on my book and was generally successful. The Voices murmured at me, but not too loudly. I finished my book and went for a shower.

Maybe it was the hot water of the shower that woke the Voices to Their full intensity. Or maybe They had had enough of being pushed into a little corner. In any case, They were at me full force as I got out of the shower, dried off, and put my pyjamas on. "Stupid girl! We hate you! Go die."

I began to cry.

Hands covering my ears in a useless attempt to shut Them out, I rocked back and forth on my bed. "Shut up! Go away! Leave me alone!" I commanded, pleaded. "Go away!"

"Go away? We stay. Fuck her up and spit her out. Look how she rocks. Baby, baby. She thinks she can escape from Us? Stupid girl, stupid girl, stupid girl."

Loud cries rocked my body. I sobbed. I was sad, I

was angry, I was desperate. "Noooo," I wailed. Rats ran around, around, around my head.

It continued for about an hour. Slowly, the Voices and rats settled. They were still there, but were not harassing me as much. My sobs quietened and I sat. I hugged my Bears to me, except for the one I'd thrown across the room in anger at Richard who had given it to me. My eyes were tired and I lay down to read myself to sleep.

Daniel came home soon after. He had noted my silence earlier and, sensing my distress, wanted to know if I was ready to talk. I shook my head sadly at his offer. Nonetheless, he sat down on the end of my bed. I started to cry.

"Oh, Erin," he said, and pulled me close. I leaned into his comforting arms and lay my head on his soft jacket. If only he could take the Voices away, if only he could banish the rats. I wanted comfort, but I knew it would be fleeting. I was under attack.

I pulled away, and hesitated. Tell him? Yes, he was safe.

"The Voices are back," I said quietly. I paused. "And the rats." Again, I cried and sought his comforting embrace. But I was out of tears. Though sad and weepy, there were no tears left. I said so, sighing. "I cried so much earlier."

"Oh, Erin," he repeated.

After another while, I sat up. "How was your day?" I asked softly.

He paused also, and began.

* * *

While staying with Daniel, I figured it out. The Seroquel tablets, and perhaps the loxapine, were laced with rats. Miniscule quantities, but nonetheless contaminated. Moreover, they were placebos. I had been feeding salt rat

193

pills to myself for most of the year. It took a long time for their numbers to grow to the quantities now gnawing on my brain, explaining the lack of awareness I had had about their presence. But now they were certainly there, and were again a threat.

I had to bleed them out. I knew that the time had come to open the other wrist. The left one still bore the white scar across it, flanked on both sides by the stitches' pale dots. My right one was pale, ready. The vein shone clearly underneath its papery thin covering.

I was afraid. Suppose I cut too deep, too far? I feared the gushing, pulsing bleed I had effected before.

I could be supervised, I suddenly thought. A plan formulated in my rat-infested brain. I could go to Emergency, explain the situation, and ask for a nurse or doctor to watch over me in case I again cut too deeply. I didn't need that much blood to bleed the rats out, but I had to make sure enough was shed to ensure the eradication of the little rodents. They came out quickly enough even in mere drops of blood, due to their affinity for fresh air. Then again, I reasoned, the more blood lost, the better the chance that they were indeed all bled out. I didn't want to risk death at all, and knew that people had died from slit wrists. There had to be a balance between rat-bleeding and death-bleeding and I just wanted to make sure I found it.

Would going to Emergency put me at risk of again being certified? I doubted it. I was being proactive and responsible; certainly they didn't put such people in the cell-rooms. I would be showing myself reasonable, which is the opposite of the irrational people they admitted to the psych ward. If I acted alone, panicked at an excess of blood loss, and *then* went to the hospital, they would likely admit me.

I had confidence in my plan. It would on the one hand rid me of the rats, and on the other keep me out of hospital. The rats usually got me put in the hospital, so if I took them out now, I would be avoiding the possibility of a hospital stay. My plan was perfect.

Chapter 15: Bloodwork, Then Riverview

It did not go according to plan.

First of all, I winced at the very thought of cutting my wrist again. I stared at the wafer-thin skin; it was translucent in the artificial lighting and the vein was pleading with me to cut. *Do it, Erin.* But I didn't, couldn't.

Of course! I thought all of a sudden as I walked down the corridor. I could get *them,* a phlebotomist, to take the blood out. I didn't mind a quick poke. I'd simply go to the hospital lab and ask for some blood to be drawn. This plan was even better than the previous one!

I set out to UBC hospital, new plan in place. I knew I needed a requisition form from a doctor for the lab to take my blood, so I headed over to the nearby Emergency department.

"Yes, may I help you?"

"I just need to get my blood out," I murmured quietly.

"Blood work? The lab's down the hall to your left." She answered what she assumed I was asking.

"No, I don't have a requisition form yet."

She looked at me quizzically.

"See, I have rats in my brain, eating, and the only

way to get them out is by bleeding," I began. "I was going to cut my wrist again, but I am afraid to. So, I just need a doctor to write me a requisition form. Please."

"Have a seat," she said hesitantly. I looked around the small waiting room. There were two others there; I, however, was the first called in.

I smiled, happy that my plan was working out. Soon no more rats! Why had I not thought of this before? Or, next time (if this did not eradicate them) I could go give blood – they take out much more than a tube or two. Wait. I'd be contaminating someone's blood transfusion. Did they screen for rats? How could they? I'm the only Chosen One, so they wouldn't know to check. Even if they did, they probably couldn't detect them, they are so small. Maybe the rats would die of starvation in the stored bag of blood since there would be no brain to eat. Or –

"Erin?"

I looked up.

"You may come in." Oh.

I followed a nurse into Emergency and he had me sit on a bed.

"The doctor will see you in a minute," he said.

I waited, humming softly and swinging my feet as I sat on the edge of the hospital bed. No more rats, no more rats. No more rats!

"Erin? Hi, I'm Dr. Phillips, from Psychiatry." Psychiatry? Why were they giving me a doctor from there? "I'm a bit concerned about why you're here today. I see you've been here before for schizophrenia and I need to ask you a few questions."

"What about the blood work? I just need my blood taken and then I'll be free of the rats and fine to go home." I

197

was getting nervous.

"Erin, I think we're going to keep you here for a short while. You are talking about rats eating your brain and that's a part of your schizophrenia."

"But you'll take my blood, right?" I figured if they got the rats out, then his reason for me staying would be gone.

"We'll do routine blood work," he said kindly. "But you'll have to stay."

I sat there fuming. The psychiatrist left. Soon, someone did come to take my blood, and I happily watched the rat-blood drain through the tubing into the capped vial. One vial.

"More, please," I requested.

"More what?" she asked in return.

"I need you to take more blood from me," I answered. "See, there are rats eating my brain and they didn't all come out in just the one vial. So can you please take more?"

"Sorry, love, but I only take what's on the requisition."

"But the rats – if you don't get them out, they're going to make me stay here again."

"Sorry," she repeated.

I was getting angry. I needed more blood out! I reached to the side and grabbed the needle she had not yet pulled out. *If she wasn't going to do it, then I would,* I thought.

"What are you doing?" she said loudly. She tried to safely take the needle from me but I squirmed just out of her reach.

"No!"

"I need Security in here!" she yelled out. No – not Security. They'll tie me up and inject more rats! Quick, Erin!

I clung to the needle over my inner elbow.

A large, gloved hand snatched the bloody needle from me. Security was here.

* * *

I was transferred that afternoon to VGH, delivered bound to the stretcher and heavily sedated. That night I was in restraints and sobbed inconsolably until I fell asleep. I was sick again but there was nobody to comfort me.

* * *

Reading my chart later, I found out that they had googled me. They were quite interested that I had written that term paper on childhood-onset schizophrenia and was now a PhD candidate under the Hospital's Chair in Schizophrenia Research – Dr. Lewisson. They asked about the paper. Yes, I agreed, I know what delusions and insight meant. But they didn't apply to me, because the rats and the Tracker were actually *real*. Couldn't they tell the difference? "That's the schizophrenia speaking," they said. That's the schizophrenia speaking. That's the schizophrenia speaking. Over and over, that was their excuse. Delusions. Irrationality. Poor insight and judgement. Psychosis. In sum: *crazy*. Locked-up, drugged-up *crazy*. *That's the schizophrenia speaking.*

* * *

"We're starting you on a different medication," the psychiatrist told me. "An older one, as none of the newer ones seem to help you." He gave me the choice of haloperidol or pimozide. I chose the former, because I had heard of it before.

"But what if it has rats in it?" I asked.

"It doesn't."

"But what if it does? I won't know until I try it, or until the Deep Meaning tells me. If it does, can I switch?

199

"Erin," the exasperated psychiatrist sighed. "There are NO RATS in medications!" All-caps, exclamation. He switched topics. "Are you still having any thoughts of harming yourself?"

They did not know about the razor blades I had sneaked in and was using daily to slowly bleed out the rats that the medications and injections and food were letting in. I shrugged, noncommittal.

"Do you have a plan?"

Again, the shrug. The Voices had a plan.

"Hanging again?"

"You're not supposed to guess!" I cried out. The Voices were livid. I put my head down on my lap. I didn't want to die. The doctor wrote: *regressing*. More drugs, more rats, more restraints. I was so tired. The Voices told me I deserved this punishment. "Bad, bad girl, knit and purl."

Then, on December 16, 2005, I arrived at Riverview in restraints, and was put immediately on territorial confinement. I dreaded the long hours, longer days, here. Soon, though, I found the puzzles and a game of Scrabble in a drawer I had never before explored, nor had ever seen anyone use.

Scrabble was to be played alone and puzzles could have no one touch them but me. Staff and patients alike asked me if they could participate; I declined. The puzzles became my world: orderly, predictable, consuming. Someone added a few pieces to my puzzle and I had to break the whole 500-piece, nearly-completed puzzle apart and start over. It worried the staff more than it worried me. "Don't look at me," I told the other patients and nurses. "Don't sit with me."

Yet, another girl, Holly, and I became friends of sorts. She was my roommate and the only patient near my age. She liked to braid my long hair and I let her. I liked the feeling of someone touching my hair. Her hair was greasy but I wove pretty French braids, which made her happy.

*   *   *

I felt fettered by the territorial confinement and asked to go to the bathroom by myself. "Okay, Erin, but come right back," said the distracted nurse. "You're doing better and almost ready for 10-minute checks."

I left. My plan had really been to just go to the bathroom, but when I got there, the temptation was just too much: I could hide. The big garbage can was positioned just in front of the sinks and I immediately saw the potential. I crawled in.

Five minutes, seven minutes... "Erin?" I crouched tightly. I love being hidden in small spaces. "Erin?" I could hear that she was looking in the stalls. She left, walking very quickly. I was, as she wrote in her notes, "nowhere to be found." Of course, I would be found soon enough.

"Erin!" she exclaimed when, accompanied by other staff, she found me behind my barricade. "You scared us! Come out."

"No." I didn't want to be out of my chosen space. "I feel safer in here."

"Well, you can't."

"Please, I just -"

"Erin, you need to spend some time in the isolation room now. Out!" Meekly, I finally gave up and followed her to the room. Later that night, though, after I had been moved back to my usual room and bed, I could not sleep. There were thousands of tiny spiders in my bed! I tried to brush them out, but then they began climbing on me. I rushed out to the nurses' station.

"Erin, it's 11:30. Go back to bed," the nurse on duty

201

told me, then saw my frantic face. "What's wrong?"

"Spiders! Can't you see them?" I pointed to my legs.

"Erin, there are no spiders on you."

"They're in my bed! I can't sleep there!"

"You are hallucinating. Now go back to bed," she said without any consolation or care. "Reality feedback given," state the notes. Dejected, I returned to my room. The spiders still claimed my bed though, so I went back out.

"Can I change my sheets, then?"

"No." I went back.

A third time out. The nurse was perturbed. "Can I at least have a shower?"

"No. In the morning. Now go!"

Nearly crying, I crept back to the dorms and spent a good hour plucking spiders from my bed and myself, squishing them underfoot. I slid out to the bathroom and quietly washed my legs at the sink. Finally, I slept.

That night, not unusually, I saw a man in the dark coming at me. I saw harm in his eyes and almost screamed. Instead, I turned my light on, and poof! he was gone. I breathed a sigh of relief. He came often, and I always believed that he was real until I erased him with light. In the hospital, though, it could really have been another patient. We were all crazies here, and I could not trust the others anymore than I could trust myself.

The ward was not a safe place. There was a player on the ward, Paul. Paul wanted sex, and he was making the rounds of the female patients. I stayed far from him and, given my cold shoulder, he expressed his interest, in vain, to me only twice. My roommate, Holly, was much more vulnerable and easy to convince.

It was rest time after lunch one day when Paul and Holly came in. I couldn't see them through the curtains that divide the room into four "rooms" but I saw their feet... and their pants, pushed down and left on the floor. I heard the bed protest as they lay down together. By now I was very uncomfortable. Having no wish to hear them have sex, I decided to leave.

"I'm here but now I'm going to leave for a while," I said loudly to the room and slipped away. I could snitch on them; I knew staff were trying to catch Paul. Really, I just wanted to leave whatever wasn't my issue alone. I had enough of my own. I did feel bad for Holly, though. I knew that she was just craving attention and was probably thinking this would provide that. Afterwards, the word on the ward was that Paul and Holly were an "item" and Paul spent more time in our room. I hoped Holly wouldn't delude herself into thinking he actually cared. I wondered, after I was discharged, how it ended. I doubted they used protection and feared for Holly's health and possible pregnancy. I wished I had thought of that in the moment, since I would then have gone and told on them in order to protect Holly. I hope she's okay.

*　*　*

Mom and Dad were in Vancouver for Christmas. They visited nearly every day and it was so very stressful. I wanted to be well for them, but couldn't. I was nearly mute and non-communicative. We hid behind hands of Gin Rummy and Crazy Eights (just like Ellen and her family, years earlier, at the NS), found the weather a fascinating topic, and exchanged awkward hugs where I tried to have as little body contact as possible. (I was still dissociating and feeling fire-like burns when touching people.)

The pent-up emotions from the visits unleashed themselves in the time just after they had left. I felt compelled to bang my head, earning me visits to the Quiet

Room and needles of rat-filled sedatives.

"Please come tell us before it gets like this," the nurses would say. I couldn't. They would just make me stop. One day near the end of my stay, though, I did as requested: I told on myself.

"I really want to hurt myself," I confessed that day.

"Thank you for coming to us, Erin," the nurse praised and proceeded to spend the time and care to bring me back to a place where I felt safe from myself. Finally, I understood why the nurses always told me to come to them. For most of the rest of my stay, I complied. "Zero management problem," became standard in their notes. I felt empowered and free, with "zero voiced concerns."

One concern for the doctors, however, was my diagnosis. I had been given various labels throughout my years in hospitals and this time, they wanted a definitive diagnosis. First, they asked me.

"What do you understand to be your diagnosis?"

"It depends who you ask," I said guardedly. "Schizophrenia, psychotic, delusional, depressed... or nothing wrong." Despite the florid nature of my hallucinations and delusions, I showed "la belle indifference" and appeared unconcerned about my psychotic experiences. I seemed indifferent, dissociated from affect with regards to my psychotic content.

"Well, we're going to have you reassessed by our psychologist." So off to days of testing I went. As usual, my response latencies were long (long enough to sometimes make me lose track of the conversation) and I tended to stare off to the left. I sat very still, and listened to the soft classical music coming from the box of crayons on the table.

There was a lot to take in when I was presented with my results. In sum, the findings were that the diagnosis was "clearly of schizophrenia to a severe degree." He found no indication of a personality disorder of any kind, dissociative disorder, nor the reactive attachment disorder of childhood that Dr. Ketch had proposed on my last stay at Riverview.

I had of course heard "schizophrenia" before (although never "severe") and was not surprised that it was most consistent with that on my files. I was more disturbed by my memory scores. I knew my memory was impaired: I sometimes even forgot whether I'd eaten a meal or returned a phone call. During the assessment, I tried to use the method of loci to remember series of words, but even this failed me. Nonetheless, even knowing that didn't prepare me for the results on my memory tasks.

My "immediate memory" and "delayed memory" were dismal. For the former, I was in the 25-50th percentile and only the 10-25th percentile for the latter, both being labelled as "extremely low." And this wasn't in comparison to the general public; it was compared to other people with schizophrenia. I felt terrible. I had always been the smart one. Now, even that had been taken from me by my schizophrenia. Then, the last line of the report: "Only with complete symptom remission will she be able to engage in optimal employment." I wanted to cry, to mourn.

The next batch of assessments dealt more directly with my schizophrenia. Apparently, I also met the DSM-IV criterion for depression, but I had heard that in bits and pieces for the past few years. My scores on "positive symptoms," "negative symptoms," "general pathology," "thought disturbance," and "depression" were all either "high" or "very high." This was also in comparison with other schizophrenics. Again, I wanted to cry and mourn the intelligence schizophrenia was taking from me.

Chapter 16: New Places For Me

Riverview finally spat me out, back to the hospital at UBC. My "Clinical Global Impression" had dropped from a six ("severely ill") to a four ("moderately ill"). One of the first things I did back at UBC was lock myself in the shower room and bang my head until there was blood all over the shower walls. I'm not sure why I did it. I don't remember the rats being terribly bad. Still, I was clutching my Bear and was clearly psychotic.

I sighed. When would I be going home? *How* could I be going home?

"I'm scared," I admitted to staff. "I'm scared of going home – going home and relapsing, just as I have been every few months these past few years." I bit my trembling lip and blinked my eyes. I didn't want to cry. But it was all just so sad, so sad.

The rats were slowly killing me.

* * *

Despite the psychologist's assessment at Riverview, the staff at UBC still saw personality disturbances and wanted me to work at decreasing my symptoms of borderline personality disorder, dissociative personality disorder, and obsessive personality disorder. That just made me feel terrible. Why was my personality – my self –

so messed up? To treat me, they gave me increasing control of my world (passes, groups), but within limits (at least, that's what is said in the chart notes). That would cure my *personality*?

So I did arts and crafts. *Leisure Group*. I made a puzzle, an alphabet sorting game, and a bobbly bead doll for my toy basket. I painted trivets with thumb-print chickies (for Marie, a friend from the lab) and ladybugs (for Melissa). A clothespin note holder for a fellow patient, Randy, who was always writing memos to himself. And a few magnets. I was very productive in *Leisure Group*. I think I was in part bored and in part trying to prove that my personality did not need fixing.

Meanwhile, I talked a lot with Mom on the phone and felt great relief and the feeling that I was not only heard, but accepted. She supported me, talked of coping strategies. It was the beginning of a new relationship with my mother as I opened up and said the things I was really thinking and feeling. It felt good.

What I admitted to no one, though, was that my bulimia still had its tight claws around my will. I would get up early, early enough to go to the hospital's cafeteria, stuff food, food, and more food down, and then retreat to "my" washroom in the basement of the psych ward's building. An hour's pass was just long enough to do it. It still gave me that high, that rush of adrenaline at first, but I soon felt miserable.

I was back to weighing myself every morning using the doctor's scale in the laundry room on the ward. Each morning I sneaked in. I was, as usual for me in the hospital, losing. Still, I was in the 150s and hated it. I had gained what I came to call my "Richard fat." I remember weighing 130 pounds on our wedding day. (Well, the day before our wedding. I was too scared to weigh in on the actual day lest the scale give me a "bad" number.) By the time I left him, I was 154 pounds: my heaviest ever. That's 24 pounds in four months. Ugh. It was even worse than being on olanzapine.

On a positive note, I was feeling well and was ready to be discharged – all those 154 pounds of me. However, I needed a new home. I wanted a bachelor's suite, just right for one. Finally, I'd be able to keep things in order and clean, the way I liked it to be... there would be no Richard cluttering, soiling, and hoarding in this home the way he did to excess in our apartment together. Discharged, but staying with friends again, I was feeling free. A week or so later, I celebrated receiving my Master's degree in Neuroscience.

*   *   *

I have been told that I have an "apartment fairy." It takes work, but I find great apartments for reasonable rents. This time was no exception. That November, after a week of walking through the neighbourhoods in which I would want to live and making phone calls, I settled on a large bachelor's near Wellington Street. I was near buses, grocery stores, a pharmacy. Rent was very reasonable and I signed a lease. I would move in January first, 2006. Unfortunately, I was again in the hospital by then – same old "decompensation due to medication non-compliance." I was, even then, still to some degree unconvinced of my illness and the necessity of the medication. Also, high levels of stress seem to bring out my psychosis, which leads me to not want to take the Enemy's pills.

So, since I was ill, in hospital, and without passes, when my parents came to visit that winter, it was they who moved all my things from the storage locker into my new apartment. On my first visit to my new home, I found a neat line of boxes and bags transversing the length of my suite. There was a lot of stuff but I knew that I had rashly taken some of Richard's possessions, too. Not important ones – unlike when he stole my BSc degree, photos, and handmade quilt – but things that had been hurriedly included among my own while speed-packing at our old apartment.

I was excited to get organizing. I loved this part of moving: deciding what goes where. I have always had, as the saying goes, a place for everything and everything in its place. It only took a few passes – which gradually became longer and longer – to get things straightened.

In the end, I found that I had several bags of junk to return to Richard. So I called him.

"Hi."

"Erin? What –"

I cut him off. All business, I steeled myself. "I have some things that belong to you. I'm going to leave them outside the lobby of your apartment building tomorrow." I started to put down the phone.

"Wait, Erin! I need to see you. Talk to you. Please."

"Richard, I'm hanging up."

"Erin – "

I hung up.

True to my word, I lugged three large bags back to Richard's. I hadn't told him the time, hopping not to see him. What I did see, though, was my bike, which he had taken to riding, locked outside the door... and I had a key. I swiftly dumped the bags, opened the bike lock, and rode happily away. Away and away. Free.

No more ambivalence, I told myself. I had a positive view of my future without Richard and was particularly excited about my new place. Mine – none of Richard's junk and mess and garbage. No more ashes burning my quilt, no more crack pipes under the couch. No more marijuana plants in the corner giving me nightmares (which happened last January). No more yelling, insults, pushes, or death threats. No more.

*　*　*

My move had placed me in a new MHT catchment area. I would now be seeing Dr. Heather Mah and Linda (case manager). I was leery, as I was of all professionals, especially given my experience at the Moncton MHT where I had given up talking because I felt that everything I said was twisted. Hospital staff had made an appointment for me to go see my new team before I was discharged.

"Erin?" A motherly Linda was looking at me in the waiting room. At my nod, she brought me to her office. It had no windows and an electronically-loud fountain that buzzed and gurgled. I sat on a hard chair by the door. Linda leaned back in her office chair and I noticed that the plastic mat under it was misaligned with the stripes of the carpet. This bothered me immensely.

Dr. Mah came in and sat down to my left, one ankle crossed over her other knee. Balancing my slim chart and her legal pad on her leg, she looked at me and smiled.

"Well, Erin, I'm Dr. Mah and this is Linda, your case manager." I stole a glance at them; I had been staring at the crooked mat. I took in Dr. Mah's perfectly-fitting clothes, the prep look with a button-down shirt that looked like a menswear one, a dark V-neck sweater, and jeans. She wore glasses, trendy, rectangular ones, and her Asian hair was parted on the side, falling between her chin and her shoulders. I waited for her to go on.

"Welcome to Willow Mental Health Team. I understand you are at UBC inpatient right now?"

I nodded. Did I like her, trust her? Too soon to tell. Although the Voices weren't bothering me then, I still had to guard the Deep Meaning. I sat there, silent.

"Can you tell me what medications you are on?" she asked, pen poised.

"Seroquel, 800 mg, Haldol, 5 mg, and Cogentin, 2 mg," I rhymed off by heart.

"Hmm. And how do you feel about this?"

"Okay," I ventured softly. Already I hoped that she seriously regarded my input.

She did, however, inform me that she would be keeping me on extended leave, which was basically being certified in the community. One missed appointment, any non-compliance with my meds and I would be automatically taken back to the hospital. That was scary.

I returned to the ward on time and quietly. As I bused up Hillcrest, I let my mind wander. I thought that I liked my team okay, thought that I might be able to trust them. The plan was for me to see Linda every two weeks and to check in with Dr. Mah every month. The frequency would be adjusted, as necessary. Dr. Mah's report reached the hospital before I did and I was discharged a few days later.

Chapter 17: Fighting "Borderline"

An appointment a month or two later was drawing to a close when they dropped the bomb. They wanted to put me in the hospital. What? I was doing so well. Apparently it had to do with my desire to bleed the rats out. I was devastated. How could they do this to me?

When Linda picked up the phone to call the ambulance, I panicked, rushing out of the office, running down the hall. *Come on,* I pleaded with the elevator as I pushed the button. I still had not found the stairs in this building. The elevator arrived and down I went, out the front door, and up Bern Street. I glanced behind me several times as I fled home. No one was following me. I was going to get away, thankfully.

I left the curtains drawn in the apartment so no one could spy on me. I sat on the couch, heart racing, reading *Psychology Today.* I was finally beginning to relax when I heard a knock on the door.

"Who is it?" I asked, as usual, as I approached the bolted door.

"It's Alisa," came a woman's voice.

"Who's Alisa?"

"It's the police," she said. They had a Director's Warrant for me: apprehension of patient. My heart sank. I let them in. As I read later, they had been "commanded, in Her Majesty's name, to immediately apprehend" me and transport me to VGH.

"You're Erin?" she asked. I nodded. "And I assume you know why we're here?" They came in and I sat back down on the couch. They remained standing. It was intimidating.

The ambulance arrived. Seeing no way out of it, I followed the police officers out of the apartment. I offered no resistance to getting into the ambulance. Subdued, I could see it would prove fruitless. Soon, I was back at VGH.

"Erin?" an accented voice spoke. It was my psychiatrist, Dr. Gordon Jukke. Another one to explain things to. I sighed and trailed him to a vacant room. He dragged my history out of me, then told me that I did not have schizophrenia but instead my sole problem was borderline personality disorder (BPD). I'd been described as having borderline traits before, but never without the schizophrenia.

He left me confused with two scientific papers about BPD. One contained the DSM-IV criteria for BPD:

1.   Frantic efforts to avoid real or imagined abandonment.

2.   A pattern of unstable and intense interpersonal relationships characterized by alternating between extremes of idealization and devaluation.

3.   Identity disturbance: markedly and persistently unstable self-image or sense of self.

4.   Impulsivity in at least two areas that are

potentially self-damaging (e.g., spending, sex, substance abuse, reckless driving, binge eating).

5.   Recurrent suicidal behaviour, gestures, or threats, or self-mutilating behaviour.

6.   Affective instability due to a marked reactivity of mood (e.g., intense episodic dysphoria, irritability, or anxiety usually lasting a few hours and only rarely more than a few days).

7.   Chronic feelings of emptiness.

8.   Inappropriate, intense anger or difficulty controlling anger (e.g., frequent displays of temper, constant anger, recurrent physical fights).

9.   Transient, stress-related paranoid ideation or severe dissociative symptoms.

That was me? Me? I thought that I met only two of the nine criteria, suicidality and binge eating, and those are certainly present in disorders other than BPD. I could concur with the various professionals that had diagnosed me with borderline *traits*, but never felt that a complete diagnosis was warranted. "Traits" are opposed to a full diagnosis; it means you display some of the aspects of the disorder but do not fulfil the entire criteria for it. In my case, I simply did not meet the BPD criteria and a single diagnosis of BPD did nothing to explain my psychotic symptoms.

A couple of years earlier, Dr. Goodwin on PAU had given my complicated clinical picture more thought. In her notes, she wondered if the childlike quality I had was not BPD pathology, but was instead a manifestation of social immaturity related to the schizophrenia. She thought that perhaps my level of intellect outstripped my social and emotional development. My psychosis had such consistency and chronicity that she strongly believed that I was suffering from schizophrenia. I think Dr. Mah stated it well when she wrote that I had a "diagnosis of schizophrenia complicated with BPD traits." I could live with that.

* * *

Dr. Jukke then decided that I was severely depressed. In the charts, he married this with the schizophrenia that so many others had diagnosed. Result: schizo-affective disorder, depressive episode. So all of a sudden, no BPD?

In any case, he suggested electroconvulsive therapy, also known as ECT – most often used for severe depression. I thought about it. I knew I wasn't depressed, but wondered if it would help kill the rats. "When I think with the right neuron, the one a rat is chewing on, it is electrocuted. ECT might kill them in a similar manner," I reasoned to Dr. Jukke.

"So you want ECT?"

"It might help," I said.

"Okay. We'll need a CT scan, ECG, and blood work. The head of the ECT program will come to talk to you, and I'll need to have the director of the hospital sign since you are not accepting it rationally."

ECT is a painless procedure. The patient is put to sleep and given muscle-relaxant medication. Then, a small current of electricity is passed via electrodes through the brain, lasting less than one second. The resultant seizure lasts between 30 seconds to over a minute. This seizure is only detected by EEG (electroencephalogram) monitoring; the muscle relaxant prevents convulsions of the body. Most patients report short-term memory loss. I, luckily, did not.

"You have your first treatment tomorrow morning," my nurse told me. "Treatment" was their euphemism for ECT. I was nervous, dreaming that night that they went about inducing the seizure before I had gone under the general anaesthesia.

A nurse woke me the next morning. "Here, put these on," she said. She put a nightgown and an adult diaper on the foot of my bed. I understood the reasons for the latter but I was still embarrassed by it. At least I didn't have to put it on in front of her.

*   *   *

ECT can be a highly effective treatment for drug-resistant depression, or for cases of schizophrenia that have a depressive aspect. For me, they hoped it would help both the refractoriness and prominent positive symptoms of my schizophrenia, as well as any accompanying depression. It is usually given three times a week, with most patients needing between three and fifteen treatments. I received three, was scheduled for more, then was told the rest had been cancelled. I did not receive the additional one or two treatments that are often given to prevent relapse. No reason why the ECT was discontinued was charted.

It is hard to say whether the ECT had any effect. I only underwent three treatments, although Dr. Jukke had discussed five with me. Why were they abruptly stopped? I didn't notice any difference in my condition. I wondered if more rats had been killed. I couldn't detect them; they were probably sleeping again. Maybe my new meds were kicking in. In any case, it was time to be discharged, I was free to go: my insight was "grossly intact" and my judgement "unimpaired." Yay.

Just prior to release, though, Dr. Jukke lowered the doses of my medications.

Chapter 18: An Experiment With Neuroregeneration

At first there were no alarms. Then it came, again, insidious, creeping with tendrils of insanity. It wound around me and strangled my mind. "Pills – let them go," spoke the returning Voices. "You are Ours," They reminded me. With each passing day, I listened to Them more and more. "Quit them." They were becoming my reality and the pills were not needed in Their world.

The Tracker had bought a new gun, replacing his rifle with a state-of-the-art sniper gun. Combined with the fact that I still had the tracking device in my abdomen, I was scared. Very scared. I still doubted he would do anything during daylight but the potential for nighttime murder was magnified. I knew that he got the sniper gun because I found three bullet-shaped objects on the sidewalk within three minutes: a piece of wood, a piece of plastic, and a short pencil, all resembling bullets. Irrefutable proof.

Pat Stewart, I found out from the Deep Meaning, was the Watcher's name. I was convinced that he was a twin brother to Jon Stewart – the guy from *The Daily Show*. A fraternal twin, but with some familial resemblance. He was in his fifties, but not all grey yet.

The information about Pat was in the *Georgia Straight*. I don't usually read this free entertainment paper but the Deep Meaning told me to get a copy of this week's issue. As I flipped through the pages, I began to see the proof. Proof of the Tracker's existence, identity, and murderous intentions. I cut out the references and glued them to a piece of paper.

I looked up Patrick Stewart on the internet. There were seven addresses in Vancouver. I thought he was the one on West 26th Avenue, near where I lived before. *I should go to the police*, I thought. But what if it was one of the other ones? I'd hate to have them go after an innocent guy. *I'm scared*, I kept telling myself. I needed a plan.

*   *   *

I am not at work today, again. I can't face those people who mess with my mind's files… reading them, taking them out, putting others in, making it all disorganized and chaotic. They know me well enough so that radio static is useless against them but not well enough to respect the sanctity of my mind. So I can't go into work while they are there.

It's only a matter of time before the Tracker shoots me or I am to finish the Great Experiment and kill myself. I'd rather not, but think of the medical breakthroughs for neurogenesis.

Now, the rats are also returning. Slowly at first, then multiplying. I can feel holes in my brain where they have feasted. As regeneration fills these areas, the Great Experiment hangs over me.

It is time.

*   *   *

The plan I devised amid my delusions involved reviewing the web pages of the Neuroscience faculty at

UBC, and choosing six whose research interests involved neuroregeneration (the repair of damaged neurons) or neurogenesis (the creation of new neurons). Excited, I drafted an email:

Dear Researcher,

I am a PhD student in the Neuroscience Program and have a research proposal for you. By way of background,my brain is being eaten by microscopic rats that live inside my skull. The issue that should interest you is that after this consumption my brain regenerates. I realize that this is a unique ability and assume that researchers such as yourself would be intrigued by this. This, along with other pertinent questions, will be answered by rigorous research. I therefore hope that you will take the time and consider this project.

In order to ensure that the rats consume enough brain for there to be substantial regeneration and neurogenesis afterwards, I have decreased the amount of medication I am taking, as the medication causes the rats to go into hibernation. Within a few weeks, there should be peak neurogenesis and neuroregeneration.

Finally, I assume that you will want both in vivo and postmortem analyses. If you are interested, let me know when you can scan my brain and afterwards I will find out the best way to kill myself so that I can donate my brain to further study. Timing will be important.

I realize this is a considerable sacrifice on my part, - but the Deep Meaning has chosen me and I cannot ignore that allowing the study of my brain may reveal ways of initiating regeneration and functional recovery in patients with CNS [central nervous system] damage in which repair is presently impossible. The personal cost is therefore of little importance in this light.

Thank you for your attention and I hope to hear from you soon.

A final click and the email was sent. I hoped that they would be interested enough to reply quickly. It was only a matter of time before the Tracker would shoot me. With their help, I could now finish the Great Experiment and finally kill myself. *I'd rather not, but think of the medical breakthroughs for neurogenesis and neuroregeneration,* I thought to myself. I felt stoic, noble, and in intimate union with the Deep Meaning.

*   *   *

My next MHT appointment ended with an ambulance on the way and me on the run.

"You're sending me to the hospital?" I was angry. I didn't need another round in the hospital. So I grabbed my bag and left, running.

I pounded the elevator button relentlessly. Linda was catching up to me – no! – and then she was there, in the elevator.

"No! Don't follow me!" I cried out, panicked. The doors opened and I fled out the front door. I left Linda behind and ran into the alley. Up to Forrest Street, praying for a bus. I couldn't go home, I knew. They'd just send the police like last time. Hurry, hurry! Don't let Linda see me. I huddled in a corner of a store's doors.

Bus! I got on and looked behind me. No one chasing me. I am free!

*   *   *

Free, yes, but what do you do when you are free?

The Beanery coffee house on UBC seemed like a good place to pass time without being afraid of capture. Being summer, there were few people there and so I found a couch in a corner to myself. The chai tea lasted almost an

220

hour, but I stayed for three. I rode the buses a while, then returned for an evening tea. Sleep for the night, I decided, would be at the lab. But where, exactly?

I peered around the corner down the deserted hall of my lab's building. No one. Should I sleep in the lab? But what if someone came in? The bathroom, maybe? I pushed the squeaky door in and glanced around. I decided on the shower stall. A brown curtain contained the area. I closed it around me. The floor of the shower seemed awfully hard. What could I use?

I ended up settled in on the lab's white coats. A nest of sorts was laid down and I curled up. I closed the shower door.

I didn't get much sleep there balled up on the two feet by two feet shower floor. The next morning was a Saturday – July first, 2006 – and though I doubted anyone would be in early, I left around 6:00 am. To the Beanery again, for tea and a nap. The day was spent riding the buses and a movie; where would I sleep tonight?

I couldn't face another fitful sleep in the shower. Instead, I locked myself into the bathroom on the sixth floor where there was a single toilet and sink, and a shower. I had a quick shower hoping no one would hear me. Unusually, I almost always kept my hygiene even when ill. It was often more of relaxation and diversion than duty. In this, I differed from many other schizophrenics except in my most ill moments.

Urges to cut intensified. The rats were multiplying and eating every neuron in sight. I slipped into the lab and went to the drawer of razor blades. Taking a few, I returned to my hideout.

I sat down on my bed of lab coats and grasped a razor blade in one hand. Deftly, I slit each arm seven times.

221

Nothing too deep; too much blood loss would drain the rats out before proper analysis could be performed. I watched as the blood beaded along each cut and trickled down along my arm. As before, I smiled to myself.

Carefully I patted the wounds with paper towels until the bleeding stopped. Then, another night on the bathroom floor. Nevertheless, I felt relief from the cleansing cutting and secure behind the locked door. Time to sleep.

Heavy approaching footsteps woke me. Terrified, I heard them stop just outside the bathroom door. I was wide awake now and mentally pleading that I would not be found out.

A radio's static sounded. It was Security! But at 3:00 in the morning? They must be in league with the Tracker! I trembled in fear. What would they do to me? Open my abdomen up with the razor blades and insert another tracking device? Then, the sound I was dreading: their hand, on the doorknob, turning it….

The lock held. There was a moment's relief. I assumed that with the light out, whoever was at the door would think that someone had locked it behind them and would go down the hall to the other bathroom.

Wait! Security officers carry keys! No! My heart raced. I strained with every shred of auditory ability to hear their keys jingle in the lock. I held my breath.

But there was no jingle of keys, and the footsteps receded. Was I safe? No more sleep after that scare. They could come back.

Morning seemed to take forever to come. Light finally streamed in. As I straightened out the lab coats I saw it: blood. My wounds had reopened as I had tossed during the night and now there were lines of dark blood on most of the coats. I swore. I couldn't clean them, nor could I hide

222

the marks. So I had to hang them back up on the hooks outside the lab. As luck would have it, most of the bloodstains were on the parts of the coats facing outward. But what could I do? I left, heading for the Beanery.

I lived like that for four days. By then, I later found out, I had been classified as a missing person. Strange.

* * *

I checked my email at the Beanery every day, hoping for some response to my research suggestion. No one was emailing me back. *Maybe they're trying to fit it into their schedules,* I thought. I sent out another email on Sunday.

Finally, on Monday morning, there was an email from Dr. Nancy Detter. She wanted to meet with me. I was excited. Besides the (presumed) interest in my Experiment, she knew me from being on my Master's committee. We made arrangements to meet. She was so eager to make contact with me that she emailed me her work, cell, and home phone numbers. What I didn't realize was that she was in league with the Enemy.

She met me in the lobby and led me to her office. But instead of talking about the research project, she began talking about the value of my life. How I could be of more service in schizophrenia research alive than dead.

Did she not understand the importance of the Great Experiment? Not realize the impact that such research could have on the field of neuroregeneration? Could she not see that I was giving up one person to save so many others?

No.

Out of the corner of my eye, I noticed what I assumed to be students waiting to talk with their supervisor. I paid them little notice except to be a bit perturbed that they would not wait in the hallway for her to

223

finish with me.

"... so this is Henry," Nancy was saying. I looked up.

They were not waiting students.

It was the police. Plainclothes.

"And this is Petra," she continued.

My heart was crushed. I knew now what was coming.

Petra spoke first. "Erin, I'm a nurse from Venture, a transition house for people with mental health issues. We're here to bring you to the hospital."

No, not this again. And worse: betrayed by Nancy. A new member of the Enemy. I slumped down in my chair.

"I'm sorry, Erin, but it is policy to have you in handcuffs." Henry said. He did actually seem a bit sorry. "I'll put them on loose, and in front of you, so it doesn't hurt as much." He snapped them on. I toyed with them absentmindedly, soon managing to slip my small hands out of them. Henry and Nancy were talking together about the miscellaneous things strangers talk about while we waited for an ambulance. Weather. Kids. Sports. Soccer for kids in bad weather.

"Hey, Erin," Henry said. "You have to keep those on!" He took my hands and slid the handcuffs back on, tightening them to the second smallest size. Ah, well. As if I could've run away with him right there.

* * *

At the hospital, given my penchant to elope, they brought out the restraints. I resigned myself to the inevitable and let them slip them on and tighten them. That is, until they came to the last foot. In a primal resistance to being restrained, I began to fight back – hard.

But in the end... the strong men always win.

Or do they? I could easily get out of the soft restrains.

224

I'd done this before. Making my hand nearly as small as my wrist, I wiggled out the fist hand. Now the second… easy. Slip the chest restraint over my head. On to the leg restraints. Hurry, hurry! One free. Last one….

Busted. A nurse pokes her head in to check on me. I stop, frozen. She calls for Security and the hard restraints. Houdini lives, then dies. Again I struggle as the hard restraints are put on. More yelling, thrashing, and crying.

There was no getting out of the hard restraints. They were locked with a key and were on one of the last notches. I had lost the struggle. Nothing left to do but sleep a sedated sleep.

However, later that night, as I twisted my hands unconsciously in the restraints, I managed to slide them out! They must have loosened them while I was asleep. I eased my arms out of the awkward and painful position the restraints had kept me in. It felt so good. After a nice stretch, I slipped my hands back into the cuffs, in case a nurse noticed and put me back in full restraints (they had kindly, at my request, undone the ankle shackles for nighttime), and fell back to sleep.

That morning, I remembered the escape of the night before. I twisted my hands again to release them from the restraints but now they were locked tightly. I couldn't get my hands out anymore. What was going on? Had they seen me and tightened them? Or, had it all been a very vivid dream? I was so sure I had been awake. Now, I doubted. The most reasonable explanation was that it had been a dream. *What a great dream!*

As usual with my relapses, when they came to the point of hospitalization, I maintained marginal hygiene and grooming. My long hair hung greasy and limp in its braids and I couldn't remember the last time I'd brushed my teeth.

Lost were my former intense efforts to avoid looking the part of a schizophrenic, dishevelled and dirty. There was no mistaking my illness now, so why bother? Even the doctor wrote: "Frankly, symptoms very unlikely to resolve, even with high dose medication – very guarded prognosis." I was "unlikely to ever repress symptoms completely with meds." All signs pointed towards "severe" and "refractory" schizophrenia.

Now, years later and finally on an effective, bearable medication, Abilify (aripiprazole), I am unbelievably thankful that there is a medication that has given me my life: quietness from the rats, the Voices, the delusions. People cannot tell that I have schizophrenia. Against the odds, I am a productive member of society and feel that my life is joyful, settled, and meaningful. It is quiet.

* * *

I began courting elopement, hoping for a break for freedom where I could obtain sharps again. One day, when staff took a few of us patients out on the attached patio ("airing the crazies" as I referred to it) I lingered at the edge of the courtyard before suddenly jumping the low wall into the flower beds and down to the sidewalk. Alas, I had leaped right beside a Security guard who was taking a smoke break. His strong hands gripped me securely and I was hauled back to PAU.

I was soon back to pacing around the circular hallway of PAU, eyeing the open door each time I passed it. I was mere seconds away from freedom. The temptation was too much for me. I took off, running out of PAU, out of the hospital, into the parking lot. I sped around back and dashed under a set of stairs. I held my breath. Would they see me? Soon I heard them coming, Security guards responding to the Code Yellow (missing patient) that was called. I willed myself invisible.

The willing did not become reality. The open stairs let them spot me and the smallest one, a woman, squeezed into the narrow and low place beside me. I wondered briefly if she minded crawling in all the bird droppings left by seagulls and pigeons. My desire to escape had overridden my disgust of the fecal mess.

"Erin, we can do this two ways," she said. "Either you come out with us now or we will have to bring you back forcibly ourselves." I cared for neither option. "Please, Erin. Make it easier for everyone."

Fine, I thought, knowing the inevitable return to the hospital would happen whether I cooperated or not. I crawled back out, "coerced to come."

It was no surprise to find a stretcher outfitted with restraints (hard, of course) in a cell. I fought but lost. As always.

Chapter 19: The 12th Hospitalization – and a Wedding

I told the doctors that I needed an operation to remove the tracking device from my abdomen. "After the surgery, I will keep it and fool the Tracker," I explained. "I will leave it on my couch at night so that he will think I am sleeping there so when he shoots me with his sniper gun, he'll miss and shoot the tracking device instead of me.

"I would do the surgery myself, but I hate pain. Even if I could find some local aesthetic, I don't think it would be enough. I'd have to cut all the way into my abdomen. Better to leave it to the professionals and be under general anaesthesia." Needless to say, I was not granted such an operation.

I settled on my bed to read when suddenly I began to hear a whirling sound. Looking up, I saw dozens of bugs flying around the room. I was terrified of bugs and almost began screaming for help. Somehow I raced out of the room, closed the door, and went to a nurse.

"There are bugs everywhere in my room, flying, whirling, so big and scary and I don't know how to make them stop, help me please." I was beside myself and almost hyperventilating.

"Erin, I'm sure that's not true," she said, trying to comfort me. I just felt unheard. "Here, let me get you a PRN. I waited, helpless.

"You'll feel better soon," she reassured me as she handed me a little pill and water. I hesitated. What about rats?

"Rats are better than bugs," I decided out loud and voluntarily took a PRN Ativan.

*　　*　　*

I was getting better. I was transferred to the inpatient unit where passes were long and the patients more stable. I was assigned to Dr. Gillis, whom I both liked and respected.

Still, I talked about everything in a detached manner, as if it were all happening to someone else. I was "profoundly flat." When asked about my mood, I would often reply, "I don't know," being perplexed by the idea of having an emotional life other than rage at being restrained and drugged and fear of the Tracker and rats. I was still cutting regularly. It provided relief from something, and by cutting, I didn't have to figure out what that something was.

*　　*　　*

My sister Kyla's bridal shower was the next weekend in Victoria, and I was pleading for a pass to go. I was on my best behaviour: no eating disorder behaviour, no cutting, no head-banging, no "agitation." How could I miss her shower – let alone her wedding to her fiancé, Simon, the following Saturday. My Dad could accompany me there and back, I said. Please? *Please?*

Yes!

It felt great to be out of the hospital. I was clean and dressed and excited as anything. The only reminder I had were some criss-crossed cuts on my arms, but I could hide them with long sleeves. It was Kyla's shower! Actually, it was her second shower, for a second wedding: she and Simon had married in China the year before, since she had returned a few years ago to teach English at a university in Shanghai while Simon finished his degree. They had wanted both families and groups of friends to celebrate with them, and the only way to do so was to do it all twice.

Kim, a childhood friend of Kyla's, and I had been planning the party by phone. It was at Kim's apartment in Victoria. Saturday morning, Kim, Mom, and I prepared sandwiches and sweets. Soon Kyla was there, and I met her varied friends.

The party continued with the usual lingerie, games, and food. I could almost forget the hospital bed waiting for my return the next day, almost pretend I was "normal." There were few rats to bother me, as I had worked hard to aspirate them before leaving the hospital. I wasn't concerned so much with the Tracker, given that I was always around other people.

I didn't think that I needed to be in the hospital anymore (although the staff thought that my insight was still rather poor), but I grudgingly returned on Sunday. The next Friday, Dad and I again took the ferry to Vancouver Island. I was so excited: Kyla's wedding was the next day. Off came the hospital wrist bands again and I was free.

Saturday morning: girl central. Kyla, her three bridesmaids, and I, the maid of honour, were getting our hair done, makeup on, dresses... it was a lot of fun. We took silly pictures and laughed a lot. The only thing that held me back somewhat was worrying whether my scars on my upper arms, my favourite site to cut, would show; I would be wearing a strapless dress. I hadn't cut in a while, luckily, and the scab on my forehead had mostly healed and was easily masked by makeup.

The wedding was beautiful, the reception classy and fun. I welled up at Dad's speech and then realized mine was next. Nervously, I walked to the microphone.

"Hi, I'm Erin, Kyla's older sister," I began. "And I have a little story about Kyla when she was three years old.

"Our parents had always brought us up to be independent and we thrived on the confidence. But one day, Kyla and I were having marshmallows as a treat after supper. We each got two, then wanted more. Mommy said no. *Please*, we begged.

"'No,' Mommy said. 'I am in charge of you and I say no.'

"'Then I want to be in charge of myself,' Kyla announced with the confidence of a three-year-old.

"'Being in charge of yourself means getting a job, buying food and clothes and making your own meals and doing your own laundry,' Mommy countered. I had by now decided that I definitely did not want to be in charge of myself – not even if it meant I could eat more marshmallows.

"'Okay. I'm in charge of myself,' asserted Kyla, agreeing to the demands. So she grabbed the bag of marshmallows and began eating.

"After quite a few marshmallows, she began to get a tummy ache. She started to cry. 'Mommy,' she sobbed. 'I don't want to be in charge of myself anymore.'

"So, Simon, I know you respect Kyla's ability to be in charge of herself as an adult, but please, take care of her and don't let her eat too many marshmallows," I said with a smile. And I stepped down of the stage and handed him a big bag of marshmallows.

*   *   *

Back at the hospital after the wedding, I met with Dr. Gillis for discharge planning.

"I called Venture," began Dr. Gillis. "They have a bed." Venture, I had been told, was a sort of temporary group home for people with mental illnesses who are well enough to be discharged from hospital but who still need some live-in and medical support. It was staffed 24/7 with psychiatric nurses, and you were assigned to a psychiatrist whom you saw every other day or so. Medications were distributed by the nurses. Passes were generous, meals provided, and groups daily.

Venture was an okay place to stay. Not great, but not bad. I mostly had feelings of indifference to my staying there. There were chores to help with, patients to talk with.... These helped pass the days but I was itching to go home. For the first while, I felt up to it, but soon things began to unravel.

"I'm going to lower your Seroquel," Dr. Chang, the psychiatrist I saw at Venture, decided with no explanation. In a matter of two days, I went from 1400 mg to 1000 mg. At first, things remained calm. Then, the Revelations began. The couple in the apartment facing my room at Venture were spies sent to tip off the Tracker. Keeping the blinds tightly drawn helped protect me from that, at least. There was, however, another problem.

The nurses continued to medicate me four times a day with the Seroquel and their pink pills of loxapine. When I had first arrived, they were indeed loxapine, and I took them faithfully, but then they switched them for placebos infused with rats and perhaps even tracking

232

devices. How could I trust them – they were obviously in line with the Tracker himself and had plans to entrap me! Especially now, when they were not allowing me to go out of the house lest I binge and, more importantly, purge. I interpreted the restriction as malicious.

So, one day, as I was called to the medication room, my patience ran out. I was being attacked from the inside. "Run, Erin, run!" I was instructed by the returning Voices. I ran. Barefoot and overwhelmed, I ran.

No one followed. I cut through properties and headed south along the quieter roads. After about 15 blocks, I sought out a shady tree to rest under. My bare feet were beginning to hurt.

After a rest, I got up and kept walking. Where I was going to go, I had no idea. The soles of my feet protested, but I hobbled along at a brisk pace. As I rounded a corner, I saw an unmarked police car, identifiable by its front-bumper reinforcement. Were they after me? I panicked and turned around and began to run. They must have seen me because an officer got out of the car and headed towards me, running also. She easily overtook me and grabbed me by the arm.

"You're Erin, right." The question was a statement. What could I say?

The police officer and her companion rode with me in the ambulance, then stood guard over me as I waited to see a psychiatrist in the ER. I was still waiting when their shift ended, three hours later. Assuming that I would continue waiting alone, they left without so much as alerting a nurse about elopish me.

This, I could see, was my opportunity. Grabbing my bags, I looked around. No one was watching. Run! I headed as quickly as possible to my apartment.

Around 10:00 that night, they came for me. By this point, I had assumed that they were not going to come until the morning. Wishful thinking, but I still appreciated the three hours I had to myself.

I grabbed a Bear as we left the apartment; one officer handcuffed me with my hands behind my back while the other confiscated my Bear. The handcuffs were awkward and I wondered if anyone – particularly my neighbour – was looking. The police car was right in front of the building. Just like on the cops shows, one of the officers pushed my head down as I tried, awkwardly, to get in the back seat. The cuffs really did make it harder. Moreover, it was more uncomfortable than I thought it would be, sitting there like that. I waited for him to help me with the seat belt, but he didn't. *How ironic*, I thought, noticing that the officer with me in the back seat also did not have his belt on.That the seat belt law was being violated by the very people who write the tickets.

Back in the ER, I was led past the waiting patients. I guessed that my previous three hours in the ER still counted. They opened one of the doors to an examination room. They began to usher me in, but as soon as I saw it, I balked. There were restraints – hard ones – on the stretcher in the room. No way was I going to let them tie me up again!

I am no longer myself; quietness eludes me, and I cry and scream and kick.

I even tried to bite one of the gloved hands.

"Hey!" he yelled at me, drawing back his hand. "You know we will restrain you. You can't win." Angrily, he grabbed my face and pushed my head violently back down on the stretcher. "You will not bite me, understand?"

"Only if you won't tie me up!"

Too late. I was restrained, tightly. For good measure, they added the powerful chemical restraints, this time including Valium.

By now, I was crying, wailing. I wanted out, wanted to just go *home* and have everything be *okay*. I was spent, no longer fighting the restraints. Just tears. One Security guard, one I recognized from previous times, stopped and looked quietly at me.

"Do you want your Bear?" he asked softly. Kindness – so rare here.

I did, but instead shook my head. Last time in ER, some of my belongings had been lost and I certainly didn't wish that on my Bear. I had requested he be kept locked up with my clothes. "Okay," he said, and left the room. Tears continued, quietly, as I lay there. My 12th hospitalization had begun.

*   *   *

I soon graduated from PAU to an inpatient ward, 2 East. There, a man was talking on the phone. He was older, frail and feeble, but his accent sounded familiar. Was he Greek? I shrugged it off and returned to my room.

Later, I was filling out my menu for the next day. As I scanned the names on the menus looking for mine, I saw it: Jonas Kopialo. Oh no...was it...*him*? Richard's father? It must be. I had not recognized him with all the weight he had lost and his thinned hair. Now I knew, and I rushed back to my room. Of all things, his room was directly across the hall from mine. I calmed myself down, peeked out into the hallway, and walked very quickly to the nurses' station."I need to talk to my nurse," I announced.

"I'm scared," I said. Trembling, I met with my nurse in my room. "My ex-husband's father is on this ward – and his room's right across the hall – and, and... I need to go to

235

2 West. I...." Words tangled with emotion spluttered out of me. "It's Jonas Kopialo; his son is Richard. Please, move me." As fear welled up, I began to cry even more.

"I'll see," she said and left my room. I closed the door quickly behind her. Wasn't she thinking? He or any visiting family could see me if I left the door open!

"There's no bed today," the nurse said when she returned. "But there will be one tomorrow."

Later, I learned that the nurse had at first thought that it was my delusional state that made me think that Jonas was my former father-in-law. Someone had therefore checked it out and found that indeed my story could be confirmed. I shut myself up in my room and the staff went out of their way to accommodate me: they brought my meals and took my empty trays, brought my pills to my bedside. I hid, so fearful, for the day and by the next morning there was a bed for me on 2 West .

I feared being assigned to Dr. Jukke but I luckily I was put with Dr. Allan. He was easy-going and careful, listening to what I was saying rather than jumping to conclusions about my diagnosis. I spent another two weeks on 2 West, steadily improving. Then, after our last session, Dr. Allan was standing up, offering a hand to shake. "I enjoyed working with you," he said. "Good luck with everything," he added, and smiled. *It was a pleasure participating in Ms. Hawkes's care,* he wrote.

Epilogue: When Quietness Came

I have been hospitalized only once more, for a month, since 2006, and spent one month at Venture. However, these stays were both for observation during medication changes to newer, more effective anti-psychotics. First was Zeldox (ziprasidone), then Abilify (aripiprazole), both tempered with loxapine. The Zeldox was a great improvement over the huge dose of Seroquel I had been on, but it gave me potentially lethal heart trouble, and so I was switched to Abilify. With Abilify, quietness came. There were no longer any rats or a Tracker, nor needles and restraints. It was finally quiet.

Yet I do not feel "cured." I feel managed, which is something I simply have to come to terms with. Despite writing this memoir, despite hearing it from professional after professional, I still sometimes doubt my diagnosis and history. *Was that me?* I ask myself. *Is that me still here, only masked or held back by my medication?* And, most frightfully, *Will it happen again? Will I lose my quietness?*

As I ponder the past instead of the future, I question how much of my treatment was necessary, and what was lacking. How many shots of Ativan did I really need, and how much was to make me a more manageable patient, an easier case for the nurses? Concerning the restraints, why were they the *first* line of treatment so many times; did no one care or have the time to talk to me before tying me up? Sometimes, I admit, I was too far from reality for that, but what about little things like keeping my hoodie on; who cares if it isn't pyjamas? Or why couldn't I sit under the "dialysis fan" for a few minutes each day? I'm not suggesting that patients be humoured without reason. Instead, I believe that letting things that really do not interfere with patient and staff safety be allowed, even if they are different.

I get most upset over the oft-repeated scenario of my pacing. In my "outside" life, I walk everywhere. It calms me, freshens my mind. So, confined to a ward, I pace; as expected, I feel soothed. But every time, the nurses would interpret it as agitation, insist on pills, and threaten injections and restraints. Isn't that enough to agitate anyone? *Ha,* say the nurses. *See how agitated you are?*

Too often, this treatment mentality is true. One of my goals in writing this memoir is to reach out to those professionals and help them see the person beyond the schizophrenia. I am an individual who can often self-soothe and reorient with my own methods. They may be strange but most are benign. Nevertheless, I am thoroughly convinced that people with schizophrenia need anti-psychotic medication. This provides the mental stability to then be able to use coping mechanisms: I take my anti-psychotics, so let me pace and I will calm. No one ever asked me about that.

Not getting my voice heard made it that, ironically, I felt more stigmatized in hospitals than in the "outside world." Inside, I was first a label – paranoid schizophrenic – and then a patient. I was sick. I needed to be controlled. I was to be *managed*. But outside, I have come across very little obvious stigma. (I say *obvious* because, given the social deficits that accompany my schizophrenia, I may simply be unaware of it.) I am very open about my diagnosis: all my friends and family, and most of the people I work with, know. They ask questions, but with care and respect. Mostly, they are curious. They say, *"You don't seem schizophrenic."* (Yay Abilify!) Yet I do wonder if they notice something not quite normal about me, and whether knowing my diagnosis lets them assume that *that* explains my social quirks.

They say that they are all eager to read this memoir. I tell them parts, stories, and they respond with empathy and concern. In fact, as I explained once about the restraints and injections and the strip-search and the cells, my co-worker actually cried for me (as did my therapist the day before, for the same reasons). Strangely, I feel comforted by this: it tells me that it is appropriate to be upset over what has happened to me. It is not my imagination that this was tough stuff.

I may be faulted for being too candid. I now cringe at the details I have told, particularly in the early years. You could say it was for effect, and it was – but in the sense that I didn't know how to respond and instead looked to others' displays of emotion to figure out what and how I "should" be feeling. This has taught me things that the schizophrenia prevented me from discerning. The smallest social graces I had to learn late, after being medicated; I can remember discovering that *"How was your weekend?"* is a perfectly normal way to talk to a coworker on Monday morning. I never would have thought of that without the stabilization

239

of my medication.

Indeed, I am stable. I work part-time at a Neuroscience and Pharmacology lab at UBC studying anti-psychotics. My supervisor seems to like having someone with schizophrenia working in his lab, and I am unsure how I feel about this. I am not afforded privileges like keys or permission to transport animals between our lab and the animal care facilities in another building... but students, transients that are there a term or two and then are gone, are given these privileges and responsibilities. *Why?* I once asked. *No answer,* he said. Is this stigma? Or my paranoia? There must be a logical explanation, right?

Before this job, I had been working on a PhD in Neuroscience under Dr. Lewisson. It had been my dream for so long. But on 1400 mg – that is, almost one and a half grams – of Seroquel daily, I could not function. I could not see how I would ever even get through my comprehensive exam. That alone would not have stopped me, though. I've proven myself before. Besides, I had a great thesis proposal (studying how, in rats, cognitive training (read: mazes) increases levels of certain synaptic proteins – proteins that are, in both humans with schizophrenia and "schizophrenic" rats, decreased.... Could I prevent or lessen these deficiencies – behavioural and synaptic – in a rat model of schizophrenia with intensive cognitive training?).

However, I began to question whether a PhD would really give me what I wanted, career-wise. Given a PhD, you generally start your own lab. Great: you follow your own interests, but you also have to oversee that lab, write endless grants and teach time-consuming courses to maintain funding.... I wanted to remain in "benchwork" Neuroscience. I wanted to work with rats and tissues and techniques. For that, a Master's degree was just right. So, I resigned. (Ironically, a few days later, I found out that I had been awarded the prestigious Michael Smith Foundation scholarship. I had to decline, but still felt confidant in my decision to leave. Also interesting is that Michael Smith specifically funds schizophrenia research, although this was not a factor in my award.)

That choice to leave coincided with my acceptance into a residential treatment for eating disorders. It would take 23 weeks for me to complete the program in 2008-2009. I continued in follow-up treatment for another year. While I wasn't "cured" (again, that word) I had for the most part abandoned binging and purging and felt hopeful that my thirties (I had turned thirty in February of 2009) would not be given over to my eating disorder, as it had in my twenties when it dominated my life. My weight came down to a level that is livable for me.

Given the length of this treatment and the resignation from my PhD work, I decided to apply for government disability. I was quickly approved. On the one hand, I was relieved: my bills would be paid. On the other, I felt like a failure. I – once the "Most Promising" – simply couldn't function full-time in the demanding work environment of a Neuroscience lab. Now, a few years later, I have re-entered the world of employment. My supervisor at UBC allows me flexibility in my hours and I am truly enjoying the work.

I remain with my MHT and have there found a therapist – who, coincidentally, works occasionally at the eating disorders residential home and therefore *knows* about eating disorders – with whom I feel able to bring up any topic, no matter how embarrassing, disturbing, or trivial. My eating disorder behaviours have all but ceased to exist. I take my medications religiously. I am breaking free.

*   *   *

A wonderful thing happened March 7th, 2007: it was time to do a load of laundry. I headed down with my basket of clothes to wash. There was a man there, too, putting dirty clothes into one of the three washing machines.

"Hi," I said pleasantly.

"Hi."

"I'm Erin."

"Michael."

"Nice to meet you."

"Yes." We locked eyes for a moment. There was something there.

"So are you a student?" he asked. I looked the part, I guess, despite – or because of? – being in my Care Bear pyjamas.

"Yes. I'm at UBC."

"What are you taking?"

"PhD in Neuroscience."

"I was in Biochem," he offered.

"Where?"

"This little place in New Brunswick. You wouldn't know it. Mount Allison, in Sackville."

"Really? But that's where I grew up. My Dad is a professor there!"

"What a small world!"

That linked us, and we continued talking as we loaded our respective baskets of laundry.

"Do you want to come up for some tea?" he asked.

"Sure." We headed back upstairs, around the corner and arrived at 309. My apartment was just down the hall, at 302.

I walked into Michael's place and immediately noticed how clean and tidy it was. Since he would not have known he would be bringing a girl up after laundry, I knew that he was genuinely a neat person. Very important to me, after living with Richard who collected every free thing he found and wouldn't clean up after himself at all.

The water boiled on the stove and he made an instant coffee while I opted for a cup of tea with milk. We sat on the couch and began to talk.

"Where are you from?" I asked as I tested a sip of fragrant tea. Still too hot.

"Malawi," he answered. He certainly looked the part, with rich dark skin and bottomless black eyes. His slight accent was warm and inviting and I began to get butterflies in my stomach. I *liked* him.

It was after a couple of hours and an exchange of phone numbers that we stopped talking and remembered our laundry. We went down together and piled our clothes into dryers.

"It was really nice to meet you, Michael," I said as we headed back upstairs. I turned towards 302.

"Yes. Very. I'll call you sometime, okay?"

"Yeah." I smiled. "I'd like that."

Michael and I have been seeing each other for four and a half years now and we are, as they say, hopelessly in love. We talk about marriage, children, the future together, as well as just relishing the moment we are in right now. He is my rock, my motivation to keep choosing health over my schizophrenia and my eating disorder. I am careful to always take my medication, in part because I don't want him to see the schizophrenic me – even though he would love me through "sickness and health." I don't want the sick role in this relationship; I want to be there for him as much as he is here for me.

*   *   *

It has taken me many years to write this book. At times I avoided it, and other times, worked relentlessly on it. I obtained my hospital records and read them with a weird sense of curiosity. Some recorded entries have found their way into my book and I hope it enriches it.

For a long time, the quietnesses that came periodically between hospitalizations never stayed. There was always another hallucination, another delusion, another hospitalization. Now, for several years, I have the quietness of no Voices, no Deep Meaning, no paranoia. There are no guarantees, but the future beckons, and I am ready to quietly embrace it.

SIMILAR TITLES FROM BRIDGEROSS

Schizophrenia Medicine's Mystery Society's Shame by Marvin Ross - recommended by the World Fellowship for Schizophrenia and Allied Disorders. "a powerful resource for anyone looking for answers and insight into the world of mental illness." Schizophrenia Digest Magazine, Fall 2008

After Her Brain Broke: Helping My Daughter Recover Her Sanity, by Susan Inman. A poignant memoir describing the family's nine year journey to help her younger daughter recover from a catastrophic schizoaffective disorder and recommended by NAMI.

My Schizophrenic Life: The Road to Recovery From Mental Illness by Sandra Yuen MacKay. "Inspirational and fosters some hope for recovery" , Canadian Journal of Occupational Therapy; "remarkably compelling", Library Journal and recommended by NAMI

What A Life Can Be: One Therapist's Take on Schizo-affective Disorder, by Carolyn Dobbins, PhD "powerful and revealing, and provides a unique insight into chronic mental disease" Dr. Thomas G Burish, a professor of psychology and Provost of Notre Dame

The Brush, The Pen and Recovery, A 33 minute documentary film on an art program for people with schizophrenia, "Educational, accurate, human, and compelling." Dr Peter Cook, Associate Clinical Professor, Department of Psychiatry & Neurobehavioral Sciences, McMaster University

CPSIA information can be obtained at www.ICGtesting.com
Printed in the USA
BVOW071249010612

291578BV00001B/8/P